Teacher-Led School Improvement

Teacher-Led School Improvement explores a distinctive approach to school improvement which encourages and supports teachers in taking the lead in the development process and offers practical strategies for managing change. At a time when schools are under pressure to implement externally imposed changes in order to raise standards, this approach focuses on teachers' ability to meet the challenge of improving schools by making their own concerns the starting point of action. This book includes:

- step-by-step guidance for tutors and teachers;
- a new perspective on the school improvement/effectiveness debate;
- an exploration of the key relationship between schools and higher education in the development of professional networks;
- a focus on teachers' ability to work strategically for change in the context of institutional, regional and national agendas;
- detailed case study material to demonstrate the impact of the approach on students and teachers;
- a distinctive model to support teachers' strategic action for improvement.

The authors draw on research and development as well as practical experience gained working with the model over many years as part of a postgraduate programme. There is an emphasis on networking, which enables the participating teachers to disseminate and share their professional knowledge and experience within a supportive yet critical framework.

David Frost is a Lecturer at the University of Cambridge School of Education and is the author of *Reflective Action Planning for Teachers: a guide to teacher-led school and professional development* (David Fulton). **Judy Durrant** and **Michael Head** have central roles in the Centre for Education Leadership and School Improvement (CELSI) at Canterbury Christ Church University College. **Gary Holden** is a Senior Teacher and an Associate Tutor for CELSI.

Teacher-Led School Improvement

David Frost, Judy Durrant, Michael Head and Gary Holden

London and New York

First published 2000
by RoutledgeFalmer
11 New Fetter Lane, London EC4P 4EE

Simultaneously published in the USA
by RoutledgeFalmer
29 West 35th Street, New York, NY 10001

RoutledgeFalmer is an imprint of the Taylor & Francis Group

© 2000 David Frost, Judy Durrant, Michael Head and Gary Holden

Typeset in Galliard by Taylor & Francis Books Ltd
Printed and bound in Great Britain by Biddles Ltd, Guildford and
King's Lynn

British Library Cataloguing in Publication Data
A catalogue record for this book is available from the British Library

Library of Congress Cataloging in Publication Data
Teacher-led school improvement / David Frost ... [et al.].
    Includes bibliographical references and index.
    1. School improvement programs–Great Britain–Case studies.
    2. Teacher participation in administration–Great Britain–Case
    studies. 3. Action research in education – Great Britain–Case
    studies. 4. College-school cooperation–Great Britain–Case studies.
    I. Frost, David, 1950–

LB2822.84.G7 T42 2000
371.1'06–dc21   00-020547

ISBN 0–750–70871–9 (hbk)
ISBN 0–750–70870–0 (pbk)

Contents

Contents

Conclusion: Teachers and the Creation of Professional
Knowledge

Illustrations

Acknowledgements

We would like to acknowledge the help, support and encouragement as well as the creative contribution of the many colleagues who have played significant roles in the development of the work documented in this book.

We are grateful to the University of Cambridge School of Education for funding the latter stages of the research and to Canterbury Christ Church University College for funding the earlier stages.

Partnership ventures such as those described in the book can only succeed when senior staff in schools are willing to take risks and adopt innovatory programmes. We are therefore particularly grateful to the Headteachers and staff in the following project schools in Kent: Angley School, Bennett Memorial School, Diocesan St Gregorys Catholic Comprehensive School, St Johns RC Comprehensive School and Southlands Community Comprehensive School. These schools not only entered into a collaborative venture but also participated as research partners. The teachers who chose to participate in the school improvement scheme in these schools and many others in Kent are to be commended and admired for their courage and hard work. They have all voluntarily taken on the very demanding work of initiating and sustaining change; they have dared also to reflect on their own values, competence and understanding and to make this visible to others.

The research and development work documented here built on that led by our colleague Dr Chris White, who encouraged and supported David Frost in his early experiments. We would also like to acknowledge the role of Jim Nixon, a senior teacher with whom David collaborated in the pilot project. His own determination to develop continuing professional development in his school provided the basis for this work. Similarly, we owe a debt of gratitude to other in-school co-ordinators and associate tutors including Felix Hatch, Rosanne Mullings, Jane Percy, Penny Skoyles and Russell Sullivan.

We want also to acknowledge the hard work and creative energy of Phil Poole and his TITLE team who helped us to set up CANTARNET, the web-based teachers' network which is central to the developments described in this book. Thanks also to Patrick Sills and James Learmonth for their contributions.

Acknowledgements

We acknowledge that some parts of this book build on an earlier publication authored by David Frost: *Reflective Action Planning for Teachers: A Guide to Teacher-led School and Professional Development* published by David Fulton Publishers (1997).

Abbreviations

CCCUC	Canterbury Christ Church University College
CANTARNET	Canterbury Action Research Network
CANTIS	Canterbury Improving Schools (scheme)
CELSI	Centre for Educational Leadership and School Improvement
DES	Department for Education and Science (now DfE)
DfE	Department for Education
DfEE	Department for Education and Employment
ERA	Education Reform Act (1988)
GTC	General Teaching Council
HEI	Higher education institution
INSET	In-service training
ITT	Initial Teacher Training
LEA	Local Education Authority
OFSTED	Office for Standards in Education
PGCE	Post Graduate Certificate in Education
RAP	Reflective Action Planning
TES	Times Educational Supplement
TTA	Teacher Training Agency
UDEs	University Departments of Education

Introduction

There is no doubt that in Britain, in the last ten years, we have seen massive strides forward in the education system. The establishment of a national curriculum and other reforms have provided the basic framework for improvement in educational provision, but at a considerable cost to teachers. Since the Education Reform Act (1988), we have seen a continuous stream of systemic, top-down change which has had a major impact on teachers' professionalism. Their roles in strategic planning and decision making have been dominated by the requirement to implement externally driven initiatives, and workloads have expanded leading to high levels of stress, low levels of morale and difficulties with recruitment and retention.

There were warnings at the time of the Act that new approaches to the management of change were needed. Jean Rudduck is one amongst many educational researchers and commentators who called for initiatives that would empower teachers:

> If we are interested in substantial curriculum change, we may need to find structures and resources to help teachers to re-examine their purposes ... and feel more in control of their professional purposes and direction. Some sense of ownership of the agenda for personal action is, in my view, a good basis for professional development and professional learning.
>
> (Rudduck, 1988: 210)

We hope that the establishment of the much anticipated General Teaching Council is a sign that there is the political will to rebuild teacher professionalism. What we are offering in this book is a strategy to help teachers reconstruct their professionalism by providing a framework within which they can play a full and active part in school improvement and school development.

Since the early 1990s, we have been developing a model of support for teacher-led school improvement with an award-bearing dimension in which schools enter into partnership with higher education institutions (HEIs) to provide teachers with the means to engage in systematic development work. The development of the model has mostly taken place within a school-based scheme (CANTIS) involving over twenty secondary schools in Kent, although it has more recently been adapted for use in the context of a number of other partnerships which also include local education authorities (LEAs). This book draws on our experience with CANTIS and in particular our research between 1994 and 1998 through which we evaluated and developed the scheme.

We believe that the model offered here has the potential to bring about lasting change and has raised standards through the enhancement of teachers' capacity to 'make a difference' in their own schools. The purpose of the book is not only to present and explain the model but also to offer a detailed rationale for this approach to school improvement, and to demonstrate its benefits and explore issues arising, through case study material.

In Chapter 1, we locate the model within the debate about school improvement and school effectiveness. We explore the way the logic of school effectiveness research has penetrated and shaped dominant modes of thinking about school improvement which have paid insufficient attention to the role of teachers as active agents. In Chapter 2, we account for the emergence of the 'reflective action planning' (RAP) model through a pilot project. This includes a critical analysis of other forms of support for teachers' professional learning.

In Chapter 3, we set out the principles underpinning the model and explain the key strategies for establishing a partnership between schools and HEIs. The model itself is presented, and we examine strategies for launching a RAP (reflective action planning) group in a school. In Chapter 4, we explain each element in the RAP process in some detail and provide practical guidance that can be used within a programme jointly led by a school and an HEI. In Chapter 5, we provide an account of our research methodology. We examine the process through which both the RAP model and the CANTIS scheme were developed and refined, and we reflect on the nature of collaborative self-critical inquiry and its capacity to support educational change and improvement.

In Chapter 6, we present a case study of the scheme operating in a single school. The model has never been treated as a blueprint but rather as a guide, which allows each school to develop the programme and use the RAP process in different ways. The case study approach enables us to explore in detail how the scheme has operated in one school, and how the programme evolved over a five-year period in response to changing circumstances. We concentrate particularly on the way in which the RAP process has interacted with and helped to shape the school's development planning arrangements. In Chapter 7 we focus on the work of individual teachers, and this is also approached through a case study. Andrew Wright has been a participant in CANTIS for a number of years, and the account of his development work highlights the way the process supports teachers in their endeavours as change agents.

In Chapter 8, we focus on the role of systematic inquiry in the process of change and improvement. The story of one teacher's development work enables us to explore the question of how teachers, by integrating systematic inquiry into their everyday practice, can bring about improvements in their own classrooms and have a major impact on practice within the school as a whole. In Chapter 9, we consider the role of teacher networks in school improvement. We provide an account of the initiative to establish a network consisting of live conferences, publication of teachers' accounts of their development work and Internet-based activities. In Chapter 10, we focus on the question of the impact of teacher-led development work on pupils' learning. We offer a framework for the analysis of how school improvement work of this sort can help to improve teaching and learning. Finally, in Chapter 11 we are concerned with the nature of the school/HEI partnership and the implications for the nature of the roles of academics in professional contexts.

One of the most significant reforms since the ERA has been the creation of OFSTED and a rigorous inspection regime. In 1995 the NUT commissioned Professor John MacBeath to develop an approach to school self-review as an alternative or complement to external inspection. MacBeath subsequently published an important book in which he argued that schools must develop the necessary skills for whole school self-evaluation so that they can 'speak for themselves' (MacBeath, 1999). We suggest that the RAP model outlined in this book could help schools to engage in such a process of self-review but in such a way that individual teachers are drawn into the process rather than made vulnerable by it.

Our ideas about school improvement are based on our research, but we would not want to claim that the process of research and development is complete. The reflective action planning model in its present form has emerged from the discourse between ourselves, our fellow tutors, the schools, teachers with first-hand experience of using the model, and other individuals and groups with whom we have engaged in one way or another. Evaluation and evolution continue in the various situations in which the model is currently being used.

We have said that we do not regard the model as a blueprint but rather as provisional proposals about strategies for fostering school improvement. We include detailed practical guidelines for schools wishing to use the process as a framework for teacher-led development work but, as our case studies show, the model is intended to be adapted to the unique contexts of individual schools and to the particular development priorities and ways of working of different teachers.

Our experience shows that where schools embrace the values underpinning the model and foster a climate of collaboration, flexibility and openness along with the provision of practical and moral support, teachers can and do take responsibility for change. They act strategically to improve their own practice and tackle issues from classroom to whole school level, leading to more effective student learning. Through strategic action for change informed and energized through inquiry and critical discourse, they recapture a sense of professional excitement and are able, individually and collectively, to make a substantial contribution to the school development process. Teachers become 'skilled in change', the prime movers in reshaping their schools for the future.

1 School Improvement
The Centrality of the Teacher's Role

It is beyond dispute that change is endemic in education although it has been suggested that change does not necessarily lead to improvement (Ainscow et al., 1994). The fact that in recent years change has tended to be systemic, centralized and 'top down' arguably stems from a global movement in which the education system is seen as a technology with which national governments can pursue their economic aims (Ball, 1999; Goodson, 1994; Elliott, 1998a). According to Andy Hargreaves, we have a modernistic education system – one which is bureaucratic and increasingly controlled from the centre – in which knowledge has become a commodity and schools are organized along factory lines. But, at the same time, teachers are working within conditions of postmodernity, with all that implies about the breaking down of traditional certainties, rapidly changing technologies and challenges to established social and economic relationships. This leads to interesting scenarios in which the dynamic tension between 'vision' and 'voice' is clearly manifest (Hargreaves, 1994: 248). In schools, increasingly we hear calls for stronger leadership and, at the same time, calls for greater collegiality, and these might seem on the surface at least to be at odds with each other; but if our schools are significantly to improve their performance in the future, it is clear that these two factors have to be reconciled.

It is against this backdrop that 'school improvement' has become a dominant educational discourse which successive governments have embraced and, some might say, colonized. The most widely used definition of school improvement can be traced back to the International School Improvement Project (ISIP) which says that school improvement is:

> a systematic sustained effort aimed at change in learning conditions and other related internal conditions in one or more schools, with the ultimate aim of accomplishing educational goals more effectively.
>
> (van Velzen et al., 1985)

This project had a major influence on British school improvement work, in particular on the thinking of David Hopkins and the shape of the

Improving the Quality of Education for All (IQEA) project which he established with colleagues at what was then the Cambridge Institute of Education at the beginning of the 1990s (Hopkins, 1987). The lessons learnt from ISIP were also very visible in Hargreaves and Hopkins's work on development planning commissioned by the DES towards the end of the 1980s; the resulting guidelines were subsequently circulated to all schools in the form of the booklet 'Planning for School Development' (DES, 1989). A summary of the ISIP outcomes was included in 'The Empowered School', which followed shortly after (Hargreaves and Hopkins, 1991); it constitutes a useful guide to the assumptions that underpin a great deal of current school improvement project work. This is simplified in Figure 1.1 below.

Figure 1.1

The ISIP Project: Key Assumptions

1   Change strategies arising from external reforms must take account of the fact that all schools are different.
2   Change takes time and needs to be planned and systematic.
3   The focus for change needs to include the management arrangements of the school as well as specific curricular or pedagogical issues.
4   Goals must not be narrowly defined in terms of test scores and so on.
5   Change strategies must take account of the patterns of collaboration in which the school is located and the roles of a variety of stakeholders and partners.
6   There needs to be an appropriate balance between 'top-down' and 'bottom-up' strategies.
7   Implementation is not enough - change has to become institutionalized.

(adapted from Hargreaves and Hopkins, 1991: 118)

There are some very useful insights here, particularly about the need to focus on the 'internal conditions' which favour change while attempting to implement more specific school improvement initiatives. However, this perspective is clearly derived from the viewpoint of a central reforming authority; why else would it need to be said that schools are different or that change has to be institutionalized? The problem is that such a perspective is underpinned by the 'organizational science' orthodoxy which is fundamentally flawed (Ball, 1987). This leads to the conceptualization of the school as some kind of mechanism which has 'levers' which can be pulled by external agencies such as the LEA.

This is compounded by the tendency on the part of researchers and other external agencies to mythologize the idea of working with 'the whole school'; school improvement projects have tended to portray themselves as being responsible for some kind of liberation from the idea of 'systemic change' by focusing on 'the school level'. For example, McLaughlin's re-analysis of the 'Rand Change Agent Study', originally conducted in the 1970s, is frequently cited in support of a claim that policy implementation strategies operating at regional or national level (LEA or district-based) are often less than successful because they fail to accept that change happens at *school* level in ways which are relatively unpredictable and not particularly susceptible to central control (McLaughlin, 1990). But we cannot assume that the school is a homogeneous organization which can, for example, enter into contracts with external agencies to bring about school improvement. The *headteacher* may enter into such contracts, but school improvement depends on the commitment and active involvement of a range of individuals and groups within the school.

A related concern is that the reductionist thinking behind much of the school improvement rhetoric leads to insufficient attention being paid to the ideological and political nature of organizational life (Ball, 1987). So, to talk of 'the school level' is still to scratch the surface of the change problem. This is not to suggest either, as much of the recent school improvement literature does, that the answer is simply to focus on 'the classroom level' (Hopkins et al., 1997; Reynolds, 1999). Such rhetoric is too easily reflected in the mantra about 'classroom monitoring' which appears so routinely in OFSTED reports. Neither is it simply a matter of training programmes for middle managers or subject leaders. What is needed, rather, is an approach which gets beneath the surface of the organizational life of the school and recognizes that schools are communities of individuals and they contain a variety of professional cultures. This means that any school improvement plan has to be based on an under-standing of these complex interpersonal circumstances. The model explored in this volume rests on the assumption that it is the teachers themselves who are best placed to develop such understanding and to use it to inform their strategic action for change and improvement.

It is also assumed here that the exercise of such leadership does not have to be limited to middle managers or subject leaders. In the development of the reflective action planning model, we have sought to pursue the idea promoted by Michael Fullan, that 'every teacher is a change agent' (Fullan, 1993: 39). Fullan based his slogan on an argument about the moral purpose of 'change agentry' which appeals to the altruistic values that brought most of us into the teaching profession in the first place. So, our concern is with the development of frameworks of support for individual teachers but ones which go beyond either mere staff development aimed at increasing the effectiveness of teachers or strategies aimed at limiting teacher stress and raising morale. It is interesting to note that the concern with teacher morale and stress is currently taking on a legal dimension with the recent award of considerable damages to a teacher who claimed that she had been forced to work a six-day week over a protracted period leading to illness (*TES*, 1 October 1999). Rather than concentrating on the issue of teachers' welfare, we offer a more constructive 'root-and-branch' approach to the problem through the proposals set out in this book.

In order to explore our alternative approach, it may be useful to contrast the titles of two significant texts which represent opposing views on the place of teachers in school improvement endeavours. One is Andy Hargreaves's 'Bringing Teachers Back In' (Hargreaves and Evans, 1997), and the other is David Reynolds's 'Bringing Schools Back In' (Reynolds and Sullivan, 1979). Hargreaves spoke to this theme as the keynote speaker at the annual conference of the International Congress on School Effectiveness and Improvement in 1998. David Reynolds, currently chair of the DfEE's Numeracy Task Force, also spoke at the ICSEI conference although his paper had been published twenty years previously. What has occurred in the intervening period is an unprecedented wave of sweeping educational reform on both sides of the Atlantic in which government-led initiatives have been dominant and teachers' voices have been subdued (Goodson, 1991). Early experiments in the development of more collegial forms of change management in the early 1980s gave way to strategies which were more directive, centralized and ultimately demoralizing for teachers (Sikes, 1992; Webb and Vulliamy, 1996; Sutcliffe, 1997; Hargreaves and Evans, 1997). At the ICSEI conference, Hargreaves argued that the post-Education Reform Act discourse within policy and research arenas has presented teachers' work and professional cultures negatively, and that government reforms have failed to build the sort of professionalism that supports teachers as 'indispensable agents of educational change' (Hargreaves and Evans, 1997: 3). He talked about the way in which OFSTED and, in particular, its Chief Inspector have contributed to the deprofessionalization of teachers.

Reynolds's paper, on the other hand, reflected the beginnings in Britain of school effectiveness research, a movement which was to provide Conservative governments of the early 1990s with the means to apply the pressure which has arguably resulted in this deprofessionalization. It has been said of school effectiveness research that it 'provides a technology for the possibility of blaming the school' (Ball, 1990: 162). School effectiveness research is concerned with the measurement of factors such as school attendance rates or examination pass rates and the correlations between these sorts of factors and others such as leadership styles or levels of teacher expectation. The availability of this kind of data makes possible comparisons between schools where variables such as the level of pupils' social and economic disadvantage can be accounted for. Local education authorities are therefore able to generate statistics which tell a headteacher that other schools with similar intakes of pupils and levels of funding have been able to produce far better academic results. Such an analysis forms the basis of target setting for the under-performing school. This logic constitutes the basis of the DfEE's policy as manifest in such ideas as 'the five-stage cycle of school improvement' and the idea of 'Beacon Schools'.

Figure 1.2

The Five-Stage Cycle for School Self-Improvement

Stage 1 The school analyses its current performance:
How well are we doing?

Stage 2 The school compares its results with those of similar schools:
How do we compare with similar schools?

Stage 3 The school sets itself clear and measurable targets:
What more should we aim to achieve this year?

Stage 4 The school revises its development plan to highlight action to achieve the targets:
What must we do to make it happen?

Stage 5 The school takes action, reviews success, and starts the cycle again:
What does our evaluation tell us about future targets and plans?

(http://www.standards.dfee.gov.uk)

The five-stage cycle is helpful, but it does not provide schools or teachers with a strategy. It is based on the logic of school effectiveness research which says that it is sufficient to provide the data and schools will 'just have to pull their socks up' and improve their performance until they reach the standards that would appear to be possible. The logic behind this DfEE contribution is symbolized by Reynolds's paper. The 'Bringing Schools Back In' slogan was part of a fast-growing response within the educational research community in the mid-1970s to the problem that was perceived to arise from the widespread assumption that schools made little difference to pupils' achieve-ments and future life chances. The legend rehearsed throughout the school effectiveness literature suggests that a Kuhnian shift in thinking was precipi-tated by the revelations in two substantial British studies: Rutter's 'Fifteen Thousand Hours', published in 1979, and Mortimore's 'The Junior School Effectiveness Study', published in book form in 1988. The essential message of these two empirical studies was that schools really can make a difference.

Prior to the publication of these two reports, David Reynolds and others had been moving towards a similar view. They had successfully exposed the home background explanation for educational failure as an alibi provided by a number of influential documents which put forward the view that the main determinant of attainment at school is the home background of pupils, the Plowden Report (CACE, 1967) and Bernstein's 'Education Cannot Compensate for Society' (Bernstein, 1970) being the texts most frequently mentioned in this regard. This notion of 'alibi' or 'excuse' is one frequently used by the current Secretary of State for Education, David Blunkett, when talking up policy initiatives. The current Prime Minister, Tony Blair, has also railed against the 'culture of excuses' which he believes stand in the way of addressing the needs of all pupils (TES, 21 October 1999). School effectiveness research tells us that schools make a difference and in what ways and it underpins educational policy which, from time to time, rides roughshod over cherished practices and challenges the professional values of members of the teaching profession. This in turn leads to high levels of occupational stress (McEwen and Thompson, 1997) and low levels of teacher morale.

The Question of Teacher Morale

This situation is of course distressing for the teachers who experience these feelings, but Hargreaves is right when he says that it is not a matter of being 'romantic or sentimental about teachers' (1997: 3); it is rather a matter of being realistic about the ecology of educational change. In order to foster and support meaningful educational change, policy makers need to recognize the vital role that teachers can play in bringing about real and lasting change. As Fullan (1991) has pointed out, there are three dimensions to the change process: the production and use of new *materials* and the adoption of new *pedagogical practices* clearly go hand in hand, although there may be cases where it has been falsely assumed that change can be managed by simply distributing new materials. What seems to be more difficult to establish in the minds of policy makers is an understanding of the extent to which educational change requires significant shifts in teachers' fundamental *values and beliefs*, Fullan's third dimension. It could be argued that if change does rest on such fundamentals, then the state of teacher morale and self-esteem becomes crucial. If we put this consideration together with concerns about recruitment to the profession, it is easy to see why teacher morale is becoming a key issue.

For us, there is no question that teacher morale is a key issue, but we are concerned that a debate couched in these terms may lead to policy initiatives which are patronizing, paternalistic and ultimately ineffective. The term 'morale' is nebulous and ill-defined, being linked to other notions such as 'motivation' and 'job satisfaction'. One difficult question, for example, is whether it is a group or an individual phenomenon (Evans, 1998). Evans's analysis is helpful in revealing the complexity of the concept but her study, located as it is in applied social psychology, lacks a sociological dimension.

Our own research suggests that the key to teacher morale is the concept of *agency* derived from Giddens's theory of structuration, which explains the human capacity to 'make a difference' through the application of bottom-up power to change the structures which constrain and determine our actions (Giddens, 1984). Evans cites Southworth (1994) in referring to the possibility that 'a more evenly distributed form of school decision-making' and a greater incidence of 'extended professionalism' will address the issue of low teacher morale. She is right, of course, but it is not simply a matter of exhorting teachers to extend their professionalism or exhorting headteachers to cultivate a more distributive leadership style. So, rather than pursuing a therapeutic approach to the management of teacher stress and the raising of morale, we need school improvement strategies that are powerful in supporting individuals in such a way that they can increasingly exert their agency and make more of a difference. It is argued here that we need to support teachers' capacity to transform the structures which constrain practice on an institutional level, and we believe that the model described in this book constitutes a suitable foundation for such support.

Our purpose in this book therefore is to put forward strategies which enable teachers as individuals to initiate and sustain change, to become active agents rather than the objects of change strategies. Our proposals rest on the following assumptions:

1   Individual teachers need to embrace the role of change agent which involves exercising leadership and engaging in strategic thinking, planning and action to improve the quality of educational provision.
2   Schools need to provide the structures and management arrangements which empower individual teachers as change agents and enable the school to derive maximum benefit from teachers' development work.
3   Individual teachers need a framework of support to enable them to engage in systematic, inquiry based development work in which individual needs and perspectives are matched to institutional, regional and national agendas.
4   The higher education sector is well placed to provide such a framework of support.

It is our contention here that higher education has a vital role to play not only in supporting teachers' continuing professional development but also, through the agency of the teacher, in fostering school improvement and school development.

The Role of Higher Education

Universities have for many years been providing long term, award-bearing courses for teachers which entail high levels of reflection, critical analysis and evaluation. The process draws upon discussion, the carrying out of some form of systematic inquiry and the reading of academic literature which leads to substantial personal and professional growth. However, school improvement has tended to be merely a side-effect of such courses rather than the main purpose. Subsequent investigations into the use of *action research* in the context of award-bearing courses suggest that this approach is more likely to be directly supportive of school improvement (Elliott and Sarland, 1995).

The concept of action research was based largely on the work of Lawrence Stenhouse and his colleagues at the Centre for Applied Research in Education (CARE). They had engaged with the problem of curriculum development and teacher development through such projects as the Humanities Curriculum Project (HCP). Experience there suggested the need for something which went beyond instruction in new methods and the dissemination of new materials. The idea of the teacher-as-researcher subsequently developed under the aegis of the Ford Teaching Project as a means of tackling the problem at the level of the consciousness of the teachers involved in the innovation. Stenhouse encapsulated the idea neatly in the mid-1970s when he argued that there could be no curriculum development without teacher development (Stenhouse, 1975). The teacher-as-researcher idea was taken up and made more sophisticated by Elliott and others, who revived the concept of action research developed and used by the American Kurt Lewin in the 1940s. Elliott defined action research as: 'The study of a social situation with a view to improving the quality of action within it' (Elliott, 1981: 1).

The essence of the action research paradigm is that the research is carried out by practitioners themselves for the purposes of improving their practice; it involves cycles of inquiry, reflection and action. This mode of inquiry seems on the surface at least to offer the potential to support change in ways that other forms of educational research do not, but although there is a substantial group of enthusiasts, the approach has failed to establish itself on a wide enough scale. This might be explained by looking at the role of higher education. Since the early 1980s, action research has been colonized by the university schools of education as the basis of the independent study element of part-time masters degrees for teachers, with the consequence that it has become rather individualistic and 'academic'. Nevertheless, there are valuable lessons that can be drawn from the action research tradition: it has grappled with the question of teachers' agency (see Elliott, 1998a: ch. 9) and the parts that systematic inquiry, self-evaluation and critical discourse play in both professional and school development. Most importantly, perhaps, it has shown how inquiry and action can be integrated into the common strategic endeavour for change.

The model of teacher-led school improvement that we are offering in this book draws upon many aspects of the action research tradition but, as we demonstrate in the chapters to come, it avoids the limitations of action research by emphasizing the strategic dimension and the role of the school. Reflective action planning reserves a role for the academics from higher education, but it is one which is subject to the discipline of partnership and the demands of the school context. It is one in which agendas for change arise out of negotiations between individual teachers and their colleagues in school; inquiry is conceptualized as the means to ensure rigour in proposals for change, and critical discourse is fostered through a school-based programme of workshops, seminars and critical friendship.

MacBeath (1999) talks of the need to achieve a balance between self evaluation and external evaluation, between support and pressure and between bottom-up and top-down development. We firmly believe that the model we present in this volume provides the means by which schools can achieve this balance. Although the starting point is the individual teacher, the reflective action planning process requires teachers to work in concert with line managers and other colleagues to ensure that their development work is congruent with the school's agenda. In this sense, the reflective action planning model conceptualizes personal professional development and school development not as in conflict with one another, but as interdependent.

2 Beyond Staff Development

Relevance and Impact

The reflective action planning model emerged out of a professional dialogue between two individuals representing two quite different institutions, a school and an HEI. One of those individuals, David Frost, was the leader of an HEI-based, part-time advanced diploma course for teachers, and the other, Jim Nixon, was an experienced secondary school teacher who was a student on the course. The diploma course had been devised to support curriculum leadership but there was a discernible gap between the marketing rhetoric and the reality of the course as it was experienced by the participating teachers. In a tutorial a few months into the course, Jim Nixon was apologetic because he could not meet the deadline for an assignment, a paper about staff appraisal; his reason was that he was extremely busy at school co-ordinating a professional development day to be held in the near future. David, as the tutor, asked what might seem to be the obvious question: 'Why are you writing about appraisal when your major professional concern is the co-ordination of a staff development event?' This question had a revelatory effect; it was the beginning of a creative dialogue which led to the launching of a pilot school-based programme led jointly by David and Jim.

In subsequent discussions, Jim and David explored their beliefs and values about programmes of in-service education and training for teachers (INSET) and later led a seminar on the subject. At the time, the term 'INSET' was used as a label for a commodity consisting largely of content-based training programmes delivered at an HEI, a teachers' centre, a hotel or the school itself. An examination of the issues explored in that seminar reveals the thinking which underpinned the pilot project.

A Critique of INSET Provision

The seminar about INSET began with a discussion about the tension between the individualistic and collective purposes of staff development. Jim and David took issue with the idea that teachers have an entitlement to support for their personal intellectual development regardless of the relevance to their professional practice, career development or school development. The

argument hinged on the problematic concept of 'need'. A series of government reports and initiatives from the mid-1980s onwards sought to rationalize
the spending of funds on INSET, and most of these aspired to address both
the personal/professional development 'needs' of teachers and 'needs' arising
from national or local development priorities. For example, according to
McBride (1989) one of the stated aims of the GRIST (Grant Related In-
service Training) funding scheme was to achieve a balance between these two
sorts of needs, but as MacLure's research showed, teachers' experience was
predominantly that of change being imposed upon them through an increasingly centralized and bureaucratic system (MacLure, 1989) which denied
personal/professional development needs.

In the run-up to the pilot project, Jim and David believed strongly that the
term 'professional development' could only be understood as being derived
from membership of a professional community and therefore determined
collectively rather than individually. However, they were also conscious of the
deep frustration felt by individuals who, having attended in-service courses,
wanted to engage with their institutions, report to their colleagues and initiate
a review of practice, but had been met by a wall of indifference on the part of
their colleagues, some of them senior managers who one might have
expected to be more alert to the improvement agenda (Nixon, 1992). This
suggested that, within the context of an award-bearing course, the process by
which a focus for an assignment is arrived at should be a collaborative enterprise involving some kind of negotiation or at least consultation.

Relevance and Impact

In the seminar about INSET, the question of what was perceived to be the
poor quality of in-service provision was discussed. This was seen to be not so
much to do with the lack of competence of the providers as performers as it
was to do with the interrelated questions of *relevance* and *impact*. The schools
represented by those attending the seminar had not yet developed the mechanisms needed to ensure that staff development activities are focused on the
needs of the participants, and that the benefits of such activity are fully realized in terms of professional, curriculum and school development. Attempts
to evaluate staff development were limited and seemingly unable to encom-
pass the idea of the assessment of impact on practice. The schools had failed to
develop effective procedures for dissemination, reporting back, development
planning and so on; it was agreed that the schools tended to suffer from organizational inertia and 'eat hero innovators for breakfast' (Georgiades and
Phillimore, 1975). It was concluded that teachers often lacked the management skills required to introduce and sustain change in their own practice and
in their schools.

Consequently, most in-service programmes had a low level of impact on
professional practice at both classroom and school levels. The issue had been

raised before of course; the James Report (DES, 1972) proposed that INSET should be more supportive of curriculum development and, in spite of a range of initiatives in the 1980s, the recent TTA (Teacher Training Agency) survey of continuing professional development still found low levels of impact on professional practice (TTA, 1997). The key question is, how could INSET programmes lead to any meaningful professional action on the part of those who have attended? Course providers have for a long time struggled with this problem. One way of dealing with it has been to follow the advice set out in the James Report and include some instruction about the management of the implementation process. In our seminar it was noted that the 'hero–innovator' story mentioned earlier (Easen, 1985) had often been used to demonstrate the need for the organizational development which must accompany or even precede curriculum innovation. However, understanding the problem does not necessarily lead to successful development work. INSET course providers have also tried strategies based on the dubious assumption that if the individual has the will and the management skills to go with it they will be able to prevail over an inert institution or reluctant colleagues. This leads to end-of-course workshops which enable participants to set short, medium and long-term targets, workshops which enable course participants to engage in self-assessment exercises to sharpen up their leadership skills, and so on. Some course providers have even adopted amusing strategies such as asking the participants to write down personal statements of intention which are then posted to them some months after the end of the course in the hope that this reminder will shame them into more strenuous action. Despite all these attempts on the part of INSET providers, those attending the seminar agreed that it was very difficult to ensure that their schools reap the benefit in return for the money spent on sending individual members of staff on such INSET programmes.

Teacher Education as Empowerment

The discussion went on to focus on the value of 'teacher education' as opposed to teacher training. It was assumed that 'training' tends to focus on the dissemination of information and what we might call 'recipe knowledge', rather than on the highlighting of issues and the empowerment of participants to reflect on their own practice or context. This view of training contrasts sharply with those put forward by Bruce Joyce and Beverly Showers and by Ray Bolam in the mid–1980s. Hopkins (1989) represented their conception of training as comprising a number of components such as presentation of theory or description of new practice, modelling or demonstration of skills, practice in real settings or simulated ones, feedback on performance and on-the-job coaching. Those taking part in the seminar had no experience of that kind of systematic training approach, but even so, the critical stand taken then would still hold for us and it is concerned with the top-down nature of the experience. The term 'training' suggested an approach to professional learning in which the sense of purpose and the initiative rests with someone other than the teacher. Such strategies are designed to achieve implementation of a particular innovation in record-breaking time. Fullan and Hargreaves described this state of affairs: 'Many staff development initiatives take the form of something that is done to teachers rather than with them, still less by them' (Fullan and Hargreaves, 1992: 27).

Jim Nixon and David Frost were determined to create an alternative to such top-down staff development events by concentrating on what Fullan and Hargreaves referred to as the development of 'total teachers' through staff development strategies which take seriously 'the teacher's purpose, the teacher as a person and the real world context in which teachers work' (Fullan and Hargreaves, 1992: 27). They wanted to see a more integrated approach in which dissemination of new ideas and practices, skill development, critical discussion of problematic concepts or proposals, and reflection on practice, experience and values were all incorporated into a new configuration of professional development activity at the centre of which was a concern for the individual teacher's sense of 'ownership'. This is precisely what Jean Rudduck had been calling for in 1988 (see Introduction).

The Value of an Award-Bearing Approach

In the seminar, Jim and David went on to explore the value of award-bearing courses. It is perhaps hardly surprising that such a group of people, being either registered on an award-bearing course or having already successfully completed one, were all agreed that long-term award-bearing courses are of considerable value. It was assumed that award-bearing courses are more likely to entail high levels of reflection, critical analysis and evaluation in a process which draws upon discussion, the carrying out of some form of systematic inquiry and the reading of academic literature, and that this can lead to substantial personal and professional growth. Participants in the seminar were able to point to examples of the knock-on effects or side effects of such courses in that they often demand systematic inquiry which in turn may support evaluation and school improvement. It was also agreed that they tend to enable individuals to become better informed, leading to a growth in confidence and effectiveness as managers and change agents. Subsequent investigations into teacher research in the context of award-bearing courses point to a wide range of such benefits (Elliott and Sarland, 1995).

However, in spite of such claims about the value of masters courses and so on, the extent of teachers' involvement in such programmes has to be considered. One participant said: 'This is all very well, but I am the only teacher at my school doing such a course and the only one that wants to.' There were clearly issues to do with access and participation in in-service education. Participants in the seminar reported that not all middle and senior managers were willing to participate in staff development activities, including even those considered to be essential to support national or local priorities. It seemed clear also that few teachers without such responsibilities engaged in any staff development activities beyond the compulsory 'development days', and that only a tiny minority participated in long-term award-bearing courses such as Advanced Diploma or Masters courses. This suggested that whatever benefits there were to be had from award-bearing courses were not being felt by teachers and schools in sufficient numbers or at a sufficient level of intensity. In the seminar, a number of reasons were put forward: only a few teachers could be funded; many teachers see such courses as lacking immediate relevance to their everyday professional concerns; many teachers lack confidence in their own ability to cope with the academic requirements of the higher education world; many teachers believe that training beyond the initial training stage makes unnecessary and unreasonable demands on their time and energy and do not accept that it is their responsibility to act as 'change agents' to improve professional practice.

Action Research and Professional Development

Finally, Jim and David presented to the seminar group their proposal to facilitate action research at the school where Jim was acting senior teacher as a strategy for supporting the professional development of a large proportion of the staff and contributing to the development culture of the school as a whole. They believed that the concept of action research offered an exciting way forward; Jim and David had both had positive experiences of action research and believed that it could offer teachers at Jim's school the means to pursue development priorities arising from their 'professional predicament' while maximizing their own 'agency'. Their conception of action research at that time was of the type articulated by Elliott (1991), who had built on the teacher-as-researcher idea put forward by Stenhouse (1975) (see Chapter 1). Stenhouse himself admitted that it would be difficult to establish classroom research as a routine activity for the profession as a whole, and he reflected on the work of the Ford Teaching Project in the following way: 'But it remains an enterprise for enthusiasts, people who tinker in their classrooms as motor cycle enthusiasts tinker in their backyards: prepared to give a lot of time to increasing performance' (Stenhouse, 1980a: 251). Nevertheless, a strong tradition of action research has been developed in the context of award-bearing programmes as teachers have moved into higher education and helped to shape masters and diploma programmes in such a way that they tend now to be more directly supportive of curriculum and school development.

Working with the Whole School

However, for Jim Nixon and David Frost the challenge was to move beyond the situation where only one or two teachers in a large secondary school were involved in action research. They wanted instead to facilitate the involvement of a group large enough to constitute a critical mass within the school. The naive assumption was that this would not only support a great deal of development work, but would also make a significant contribution to the development of the culture of the school as a whole. However, the question of the effect the project might have on the school as a whole was problematical from the beginning. A major difficulty with action research based development initiatives is that they tend to be individualistic, simply because they begin with the individuals who happen to have volunteered; action research emphasizes the autonomy and subjectivity of the individual action researcher. The question was how to match the needs of the individual and the needs of the institution. On the one hand, the individual teacher has professional and academic concerns which are determined in part by the individual's biography, their vested interests, their values and their conception of good professional practice. These concerns are also embraced by the individual's need for self-actualization, the need to express and develop their point of view. On the other hand, there are the policy imperatives of the institution, the vested interests of various groups and individuals within the power structure of the school and the priorities determined by the apparatus for corporate planning within the institution. Action research was seen not as a solution but as a convenient tool. Jim and David had first-hand experience of it; they understood it and believed that it had the potential to make a significant impact on the professional development of the participants and on curriculum development throughout the school.

Of course there were alternative ways of thinking about supporting inquiry and reflection in schools, and there were models available which seemed on the face of it at least to be far more whole school focused. For example, the GRIDS (Guidelines for Review and Internal Development in Schools) approach involved the whole school in a rational and managed developmental process (Abbott et al., 1988). This approach places inquiry and reflection in support of curriculum development squarely in its institutional setting, and the review process would normally be facilitated by outside agencies or consultants. The insights gathered through the use of GRIDS were incorporated into later work on school development planning, given official backing and enshrined in documentation which carries the DES stamp of approval (DES, 1989; Hargreaves and Hopkins, 1991). However, this approach was seen as managerialist, hierarchical (Elliott, 1993b) and based on a flawed 'organizational science'-based conception of the way schools actually operate (Ball, 1987). In contrast to this, action research did not rest on the idea of the school as a rational system, but rather as a political system within which there is scope for individuals to make a difference through critical inquiry.

In the early part of 1991, Jim and David began to explore with their respective institutions the possibility of creating an award-bearing programme which would be more directly supportive of development work in schools, one which would operate on the school site and would be jointly led by the school and the HEI. Jim's headteacher was prepared to support the project on the understanding that the school would benefit and the project was recognized as having benefits which go far beyond support for curriculum development. In an interview during the first year of the project, the head made the following statement:

> I believe that teachers are professionals and should be self-reflective practitioners. The more we can do to encourage them to step back, look at their role and analyse it, the better. It leads to better teaching and, in the end, the kids benefit.

It was assumed that the school was prepared to back the project because of the obvious implications for the culture of the school as an organization.

Launching the Pilot Project

A close collaboration between the two institutions would address some of the school's development priorities in a way that would lead to further professional qualifications for the dozen or so participating teachers. Jim Nixon and David Frost would be co-tutors on a bespoke award-bearing programme, and all members of staff would be invited to apply to the headteacher for a free place. The introduction of the project was supported by a brochure the central message of which hinged on four key words: *recognition, support, enhancement* and *accreditation*.

It was put to colleagues that they were the unsung heroes of curriculum development. Most of them were engaged in hard work which generated results which in other contexts would be dignified by terms such as 'study' and 'research'. It was time that this valuable work was made visible and due credit given. It was also put to colleagues that innovation and development were often thankless tasks which resulted in feelings of isolation and frustration. The proposed programme offered the possibility of support through membership of a curriculum research and development support group. Within this group, protected as it would be by rules of confidentiality, individuals could share their problems and derive much needed succour. The third principle was concerned with the idea of enhancing the development work normally undertaken by providing a structured framework and criteria against which to judge the outcomes. This suggested a process model in which teachers would be offered the challenge and critique which would make the research and development work more rigorous. Finally, Jim and David put forward the notion that they were offering a means by which colleagues could put forward evidence of their research and development work in order to claim credit towards a diploma and subsequently an MA in curriculum development.

In practical terms, this meant a series of monthly 'twilight' sessions held at the school and jointly led by the HEI tutor and the in-school tutor. Reports of inquiry-based curriculum development work would be assembled in the form of a curriculum development portfolio. The portfolio idea was a key element, and it underwent radical development within the first year of the project.

The rationale for the project together with its aims were included in the guidance material provided for the participants at the start of the project. The aims of the project were expressed as wanting to support curriculum and professional development in order to enhance the quality of learning experienced by students. Specifically the project would:

- provide a framework for colleagues' professional action plans;
- support and encourage collaborative action research;
- enable colleagues to develop their capacity for reflective practice;
- provide opportunities for debate and discussion about the curriculum;
- enhance colleagues' career development through the recognition of professional learning and development work.

The Aim of Empowerment

Looking back on the project a year later, David characterized the aims in the following way:

> the empowerment of teachers and the promotion of a range of values related to reflective practice, professional collegiality, and the development of critical pedagogy. Through our dialogue about professional development and school improvement we had been able to articulate for ourselves a set of values which, if fully realized in practice would lead to a range of outcomes which are centrally concerned with the empowerment of teachers to:
>
> - develop their capacity for curriculum debate;
> - develop their self-awareness and sense of professional growth;
> - increase their ability and motivation to engage in curriculum decision-making;
> - increase their capacity for honest self-evaluation;
> - develop a critique of educational policies at both local and national levels;
> - increase their ability to build and test theories about teaching and learning.
>
> (Frost, 1993: 13)

To some observers, this aim of *empowering* colleagues in the school may seem to represent a contradiction. It is assumed by many that he who pays the piper calls the tune. Holly, for example, has argued that action research and schools have 'dichotomous, polar tendencies': 'Action research fosters collegiality, informality, openness and collaboration across boundaries, etc. while institutions veer towards the hierarchical, bureaucratic and formal' (Holly, 1984: 100). More recently, it has been suggested that the term 'empowerment' is an unhelpful distraction and that the very concept means many different things to many different people. Fielding's (1996) worst fears seem to be that its use may well indicate that those in a position to 'empower' aim to retain the 'dependency and domination' on which they thrive. This critique is helpful in that it challenges us to problematize our aims and to raise questions about the extent to which the strategies we developed really do address issues of power. As an external agent, an HEI tutor could hardly be accused of withholding power or merely dispensing measured doses as a palliative to keep the wheels of industry turning, but in the long run we were forced to address the question of how this emancipatory rhetoric may have served a legitimating function in a process which could still be described as imperialistic.

Issues concerned with power and its use in relation to our project were discussed at a formal level. When the project was first floated, it was suggested by one of the university members of the Board of Examiners that the location of the project within the single school might be an inhibiting factor. It was suggested, for example, that the role of tutor being assumed by the school's staff development co-ordinator might compromise academic freedom and turn the course into a tool of senior management manipulation.

The response to such challenges was to set about the building of safeguards which would promote academic freedom and offset the power advantage that the school had through its control of funding. First, there was the development of an ethical framework for the project; second, there was the clear separation between the role of tutor and any management role that the tutors might otherwise occupy; and third, there was the research perspective adopted by the project leaders.

The Ethical Framework for Action Research

At the outset of the project, the participants expressed concerns about the extent of their freedom in respect of data gathering and the confidentiality within group discussions. The tutors had demanded that these discussions should be regarded as confidential, but what about the school's right to know? The participants themselves were quite anxious about this. One member of the group said that her head of department had already demanded that any data-gathering exercise should be approved by him in advance, and that he should have the right to have first sight of any data collected. Another senior manager had demanded the right to see any papers the participants wrote in the context of the project. After discussion with the group, we drew up a list of ethical principles to which we asked the senior management team to agree. The list of principles guaranteed confidentiality and gave participants control over their data gathering and their portfolios. They also protected their right to engage in critical discussion of policies and practice within the school (see Chapter 3 for a complete list). The agreement to these principles provided everyone involved in the project with a clear framework for action and, as a result, participants felt considerably safer. It was also believed that colleagues outside the project would be reassured about the gathering and use of data. This optimistic view was reinforced when the participants were interviewed as part of the evaluation of the project.

The Role of the Tutor

An essential part of this ethical dimension was the question of the roles of the tutors and those of the managers who had oversight of the work of the project. Jim Nixon and David Frost acted as co-tutors with complementary areas of experience and expertise. Being tutors meant that they were to restrict their roles to leading seminars, running workshops and providing tutorial guidance on the *process* of inquiry and reflection. The role did not include advising the teachers on curricular, pedagogical or management matters, nor did it include giving or withholding approval in relation to the focus of teachers' inquiries or the aims of whatever development work they were contemplating. In the early stages of the project, participants would approach the tutors and say something like: 'I am thinking of trying to develop a conservation pond to support teaching in the science department; do you think that would be a good idea?' The tutor's response would always be to say that his opinion is irrelevant because the question of whether there is a need for a conservation pond and how it could be used in the curriculum is a matter for the school as an organization, and therefore the proposal should be set out in a personal development plan or a departmental discussion document and become subject to negotiation, consultation and discussion. The school had a 'line management' system, so the tutors developed strategies to promote such negotiation and tried also to provide support for those outside our group who were likely to be approached in their role as 'line manager'. The process at the core of the project demanded that participants consult with their line manager about the focus of their development work. The intention was to stimulate a dialogue between teachers in the school. It was clearly more problematic but nonetheless important for Jim to remain detached from the policy questions embedded in the participants' proposals. The tutor's role in this situation was to become a 'critical friend' who could advise and challenge colleagues in terms of their inquiry strategies, their analysis and the presentation of their ideas. It was for the participants' line managers who were not directly involved in the project to agree on the validity of the focus of the participants' work. It was significant that Jim was not then a member of the senior management team, and this raises the question of whether senior managers could ever adopt a plausible 'critical friend' role within their own schools.

Adopting a Research Perspective

The guidance material issued to all participants at the start of the programme included the following statement:

> The scheme is also framed as research and will therefore be the subject of monitoring and evaluation which will enable the school and the HEI to develop:
>
> (a) new understanding about the possibilities for school-based professional development, and
> (b) more effective strategies for the management of professional development in schools.

Stenhouse's simple statement that research is 'systematic inquiry made public' had been used to promote action research within the school and so, by the same token, the project leaders felt an obligation to take steps to make their own work visible and to generate discussion about the project (Stenhouse, 1980b). Evidence gathering procedures were set up and a 'steering group' established to consider the issues emerging in the early stages. This early evaluation led to immediate changes such as the reconstruction of the idea of the portfolio as a collection of evidence arising from a systematic process which we referred to as 'reflective action planning'. In essence, the programme provides support and guidance which enables participants to build up evidence of their curriculum development work in a piecemeal way. Personal development plans, action plans, audit exercises, departmental discussion papers and other artefacts are assembled together with critical narrative writing and commentary to form a coherent portfolio which can be examined as a module within the HEI's advanced diploma programme.

From Pilot Project to School Improvement Scheme

For Jim and David, the pilot was in its early stages and there were many issues yet to be addressed, so they did not want to consider replicating the project in other schools. However, there were other factors which helped to shape events. The recruitment of the maximum number of students was considered essential to the HEI's long term goal of achieving university status, and this pilot project opened a window of opportunity. Earlier in that academic year the DFE had issued Circular 9/92, which had set out the requirement that PGCE courses were to become more school-based with a substantial proportion of the funding to be transferred to the schools (DFE, 1992). The discussions within the HEI's Education Department and with senior management throughout that academic year centred on how the institution might replace the income which would be lost because of the transfer of funds to the schools and so avoid the need to make teaching staff redundant. The pilot project, problematic as it was, nevertheless demonstrated that, through the setting up of school-based in-service programmes in partnership with schools, it was possible to recruit a much greater number of students than through traditional in-service award-bearing courses. It was therefore decided, at senior management level, to replicate the project as soon as possible.

Principles of Procedure

The pilot project was born out of certain beliefs and value positions which the two collaborators held in common (see Nixon, 1992). They developed and rehearsed these shared values and beliefs about their work through an ongoing dialogue and these formed the criteria for judgement as the scheme was evaluated and developed. However, in extending the collaboration there was a clear need for a more coherent and detailed expression of principles which could be shared and developed in collaboration with colleagues who had become involved in tutoring on the expanded scheme. The term 'principles of procedure' is one which Stenhouse took from R.S. Peters and used to mean those criteria which determine validity in an educative process (Stenhouse, 1975). There is always a danger in any systematic approach that the technology involved – in this case, it is mostly embodied in a 'portfolio guidance booklet' – can become a stultifying straitjacket which undermines tutors' and participants' sense of ownership. David Frost firmly believed that the scheme could only move forward as a team effort which necessarily entailed the development of shared values and practices (see Rudduck, 1991; Fullan, 1993). Statements about principles of procedure do not dictate particular pedagogic strategies, nor do they specify particular learning outcomes; instead they provide a set of process criteria which can be debated and used to evaluate particular strategies. Set out below is a list of the principles of procedure agreed as a working framework at the first meeting of the research group set up to evaluate and further develop the proposed school-based scheme.

Figure 2.1

Principles of Procedure for a School–Based Programme

A school-based, award-bearing, school improvement programme is likely to be successful if it:

- is tutored collaboratively by a member of the school staff and a tutor from an HEI;
- is conducted in a fully equipped seminar room on the school premises or other convenient site;
- provides support and sanction for open-ended inquiry;
- provides a framework of guidance for individuals' professional action planning;
- facilitates the matching of individuals' action planning to the school's development priorities;
- is supported by the management arrangements of the school;
- provides a confidential forum for critical analysis of curricular issues;
- challenges participants' assumptions about educational issues;
- demands rigour in participants' professional inquiries;
- facilitates the recognition of individuals' professional achievement;
- supports the use of inquiry strategies which make a good fit with teachers' professional work;
- values and accepts piecemeal evidence of systematic curriculum development work;
- provides guidance and clarification about the nature of evidence of action planning, development work, inquiry and critical reflection;
- engages teachers in critical dialogue with their line managers about curricular and professional issues;
- facilitates career development through the award of further professional qualifications;
- encourages teachers to take responsibility for their own professional learning;
- provides an ethical framework for the development of critiques of educational policies at both local and national levels;
- empowers teachers to benefit from and contribute to wider educational discourse.

These principles of procedure were developed through discussion with critical friends and disinterested scrutineers, and used to guide the operation of the approach in a number of other schools. The HEI elected to build on the pilot project to develop a scheme in which all large schools in the county would be invited to participate. Many of the secondary schools in Kent had opted for 'grant maintained' status and were keen to reduce their dependence on the LEA for support. The proposed 'reflective action planning' scheme, referred to here as the CANTIS (Canterbury Improving Schools) scheme offered an attractive alternative, and so by the beginning of the 1993–4 academic year there were RAP (reflective action planning) groups established in at least ten schools.

3   Establishing School–University Partnerships for School Improvement

In Chapter 2 we explained how the ideas underpinning this approach to school improvement were developed through a pilot project. This led to the conception of the reflective action planning process as a model for teacher-led school improvement. In this chapter, we set out the fundamental principles underpinning the model. We outline ways in which the school/HEI partnership can be established, and suggest strategies for the setting up of a RAP (reflective action planning) group in a school. In Chapter 4 we will consider each element of the process in detail.

Evidence from the scheme operating in Kent schools (gathered primarily in the course of the ESACS Project, see Chapter 4) shows that participants experience a wide range of benefits as a result of their involvement. They have enhanced opportunities for professional learning, including input from the group sessions, guided reading and systematic research around their chosen focus, increased networking within and beyond the school, development of professional competence (for example, through leading sessions, reporting to different audiences, experimenting with pedagogy), and greater self-awareness through a more reflective approach to practice and through critical feedback from colleagues. They frequently describe an increase in confidence and self-worth as commitment and expertise in a particular curriculum area becomes known and is often recognized formally by the school through promotion or the allocation of additional responsibilities. This is accompanied by a generally higher profile amongst the staff, with an increased ability and willingness to express ideas and opinions and a greater feeling of autonomy. The individual voice is strengthened by the power of systematic inquiry in providing a strong basis of evidence for effecting change. As they become more established as members of the group and more experienced in the reflective action planning process, participants begin to see themselves increasingly as change agents in the context of the school development process as a whole, valuing the support of the group in providing a positive and confidential forum for testing ideas and discussing issues and problems.

Finally, a recurring theme in evaluations of the model is the extent to which the programme provides stimulation, challenge, enjoyment and motivation which inspires participants in their everyday work. While much staffroom discourse is problem-orientated and maintenance-driven and meetings tend to be taken up with information exchange and externally prescribed agendas, the reflective action planning groups are a non-hierarchical setting for debate about educational issues, for exploring personal professional values and concerns, for being *allowed* to share and celebrate the joys and successes as well as the problems of being a teacher and being a learner. While many teachers cite their ambition to achieve further qualifications as their original reason for joining an accredited programme, it is the support and inspiration for professional practice and the sense of belonging to a learning community which continue to draw them to attend twilight meetings at the end of a full day's teaching and to maintain the additional commitment of leading inquiry-based development work.

One group within the CANTIS scheme, comprising teachers from a number of different schools, experienced in reflective action planning, found that Friday was the only viable day in their busy schedules. They consistently attended group meetings from 4.30 p.m. to 6.30 p.m. in the host school, as their colleagues hastened home for the weekend. They arrived tired and tended to want to unburden themselves of their everyday concerns over tea and biscuits before embarking upon the agenda for the session. They (and their tutors) left refreshed, challenged and inspired by the depth of discussion and involvement engendered by a programme built around their own professional agendas, interests and expertise within the context of the wider educational discourse. Most have maintained their involvement in this professional network following the completion of their masters degrees, by attending conferences, visiting other groups to lead sessions, writing for publication, becoming associate tutors running their own reflective action planning groups, pursuing further academic qualifications or simply maintaining informal contacts. They show that this approach to school improvement becomes integral to professional practice. It reaches far beyond the award-bearing dimension to provide a framework for an extended professionalism (Stenhouse, 1975) which involves the development of situational understanding (Elliott, 1993a) and improvement in practice as continual processes. It supports and enhances the agency of individual teachers and extends their capacity to manage change and to drive school improvement.

Fundamental Principles

The research built into the pilot scheme led to the development of a set of 'principles of procedure', set out in full at the end of Chapter 2, which were used as a basis for further development of the model. These principles of procedure can be summarized in the form of three overarching principles: the principle of *partnership*, the principle of *school improvement* and the principle of *critical discourse.* We offer them here as a basis for agreement between schools and HEIs who wish to establish RAP groups.

1   *The principle of partnership.* It is essential that such school-based programmes are designed and led collaboratively, with the HEI and the school being equal partners. The HEI tutor should work with an 'in-school co-ordinator' who is an experienced teacher within the project school. The in-school co-ordinator might also be designated an 'associate tutor' by the HEI if he or she has the necessary qualifications, experience and inclination. Such a partnership is able to draw upon both external and internal knowledge. This facilitates discourse which is both relevant and critical; relevant in that it focuses on matters which are of direct concern both to the school as an organization and to individual participants, and critical in that it is informed by conceptual analysis and research findings from the literature and contrasting accounts of practice elsewhere.

2   *The principle of school improvement.* It is essential that the work, for which participants earn credit within the award-bearing framework, should arise from personal development priorities which match or reflect the school's priorities. This principle demands firstly, a process of personal reflection in which the individual participant clarifies their professional values and vision and identifies personal development priorities, and, secondly, a process of negotiation and consultation in which the individual tries to seek agreement with colleagues as to the appropriateness of their priorities and plans. It is essential that inquiry tasks are not conceived merely as 'doing a research project', but rather as improving an aspect of practice through a systematic, planned and managed process of inquiry-based development work.

3   *The principle of critical discourse.* The fundamental purpose of the process is to support school improvement, but this depends on a conception of professionalism in which teachers see themselves as engaging in critical discourse as members of a professional community which extends beyond the particular school and beyond the boundaries created by regional or national policies. Participation in critical discourse is facilitated through membership of a RAP group, reading, reflection, data analysis and critical narrative writing. Critical discourse also takes place in the daily transactions between participants and their colleagues as they engage in everyday deliberation and decision making and pursue their development goals. This discourse can be enhanced by supporting teachers as change agents and it can be enriched and extended through membership of external networks.

We suggest that, if the principles set out above are accepted as common ground between those wishing to form a partnership to support teacher-led school improvement, they could be used as a basis for a presentation to the teachers in schools where the model is being considered as a possible way forward. The following list of 'key strategies' expresses the same ideas but in a more concrete form.

Key Strategies

1 The school invites members of staff to play an active part in development work and review their management arrangements to ensure that 'change agents' have opportunities to exercise leadership.
2 Participants are provided with a framework of support for systematic, inquiry-based development work.
3 Participants are expected to engage in 'personal vision-building' (Fullan, 1993) and to make their priorities explicit in the form of a personal development plan which can be shared with colleagues and negotiated in the context of the school's development agenda.
4 Participants are expected to plan their interventions systematically and make their intentions explicit in the form of written action plans which can be negotiated with colleagues and other key stakeholders within the school.
5 Critical discourse is fostered and guidance provided through the provision of a jointly planned and led programme of twilight workshops/seminars.
6 Independent work is supported through the provision of a booklet containing guidelines, formats and facsimiles of teachers' planning documents and through the provision of individual tuition.
7 Critical discourse and the sharing of ideas are fostered through membership of regional, national and international networks, ideally including a dedicated network of participants from other schools.
8 Participants are expected to keep a portfolio of evidence of the development work together with explanatory commentary so that the process is fully documented and can be reviewed with colleagues.
9 Participants are invited to reflect on the process of change and to analyse it in the form of a critical narrative which is added to the portfolio for the purposes of a deeper reflection supported by academic tuition.
10 Participants are invited to present their portfolios to the HEI for assessment for the purposes of accreditation.

These strategies are represented in the form of a diagram (Figure 3.1). The process is not as linear and compartmentalized as the diagram might suggest of course; it is complex and organic, but representing it in this way helps potential participants and their schools to think about the elements of the change process and to develop their understanding of it as a whole.

Forming a Partnership

The reflective action planning model was originally devised in the context of a partnership between schools and HEIs, but more recently it has also been used within a three way partnership which includes an LEA. For the purposes

Figure 3.1 *A Process for Teacher-Led School Improvement: The Reflective Action Planning Model*

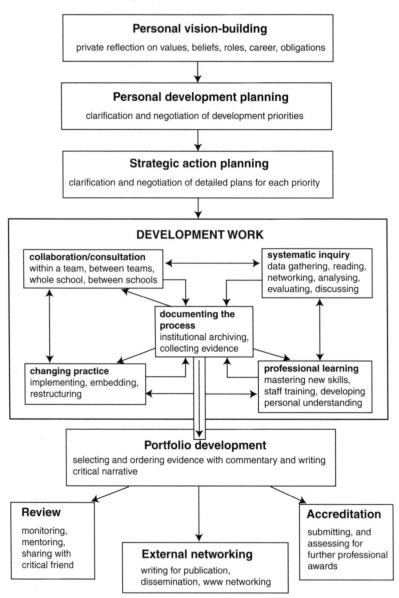

Note: This model represents a process through which individual teachers can 'make a difference'; the outcomes of the process are changes in practice within the school, the professional development of individual teachers and their colleagues, and the development of the school as an organization.

of the guidelines set out here, it is assumed that the external agency is an HEI, but there is no reason why the partnership should not include an LEA.

It is essential to the model that the process is supported both by the individual's school and by an external agency working in close collaboration. This partnership is represented by two key people, the 'in-school co-ordinator' and the 'tutor'. The in-school co-ordinator is a designated member of staff within the school who has the ability to co-ordinate and sufficient seniority or position to ensure that the programme is adequately resourced. The tutor is a member of the HEI staff or is appointed by the HEI to act as an associate and is able to facilitate access to a good library and research networks. This is the essential working relationship on which the programme depends. It is therefore vital that the individuals designated by the two institutions are the right people for the task, and that they are accepted as such not only by the two contracting institutions but also by the participants. It is up to the individuals concerned to negotiate between themselves the precise division of labour and the nature of their respective roles.

The initiative for a RAP programme or scheme might come from a school which approaches an HEI with a request for support for school improvement. Alternatively, it might come from an HEI seeking new roles in continuing professional development. Since the abolition of 'grant maintained' status for schools and the strengthening of the LEAs' role in school improvement, the initiative might come from an LEA which seeks to raise standards in schools by providing such a scheme. Whatever the case, it is important that each partner is clear about the contribution they will make to the operation of the programme and that these understandings are clearly specified in a contract or memorandum of agreement between the two institutions. A contract of this sort would have to be based on a joint view of matters such as the financial viability of the proposed programme and the level of acceptance of the proposal on the part of members of the school staff.

The School's Role

It is essential that the school plays a full part in supporting the RAP process. This means that the senior management team must ensure that there is widespread agreement about the decision to establish a RAP group within the school and that the 'management arrangements' (Hargreaves and Hopkins, 1991) do not present an insurmountable obstacle. The following points could be used as a checklist:

1   The school should designate a suitable member of staff as the in-school co-ordinator. This needs to be someone who is a member of, or has access to, senior management in order to be able to command relevant resources, facilitate adequate communication and ensure that the work

has maximum impact on the school as a whole. However, there is a danger that too much seniority can inhibit participants.

2   The school should ensure that the project is resourced adequately in terms of the appropriateness of the group leaders, the quality of the accommodation, the adequacy of the time allocation, the provision of audio visual equipment, refreshments and other practical requirements.

3   The school should ensure that participants have opportunities for consultation and negotiation with key individuals and groups within the school (for example, mentor, team leader, line manager, critical friend, appraiser) and that these key individuals are fully informed about their role in the process.

4   The school should ensure that the development planning process is sufficiently open and flexible to allow for participation of teachers, whatever their status or position within the school.

5   The school should ensure there is good liaison and collaboration between the school and the HEI or other external agency involved, particularly for the purposes of quality assurance and maintaining the viability of the group through ongoing recruitment and adaptation to changing circumstances.

The HEI's Role

The most important and over-arching need is to ensure that the HEI personnel involved both understand and are fully committed to the fundamental principles and purposes of the scheme. The following points could be used as a checklist:

1   The HEI should ensure that a suitable member of staff is designated as the tutor. This needs to be someone who has experience of supporting practitioner research and school improvement activity.

2   The HEI should ensure the provision of effective guidance material to support the reflective action planning process. This can be adapted from what is published here and elsewhere (Frost, 1997).

3   The HEI should ensure that the tutor collaborates with the in-school co-ordinator to plan and lead a programme of seminars and workshops to support the RAP process and provide input on subject matter which is of most value to the members of the group.

4   The HEI should ensure the provision of individual tutorial support appropriate to the level of accreditation sought.

5   The HEI should ensure that there is access to literature.

6   The HEI should ensure that professional networking is facilitated and encouraged.

We cannot emphasize enough that the partnership between the school and the HEI should be an equal one and that the in-school co-ordinator needs to have sufficient personal strength and authority to be able to ensure that the school plays a positive role in the pursuit of the goals outlined above.

The Role of the Associate Tutor

The concept of the associate tutor first developed during the planning of the pilot project as a way of achieving a shared perspective within the partnership. It was intended that the HEI tutor and the teacher collaborator or in-school co-ordinator would make links with one another's institutions so as to maintain an appropriate level of discourse and develop their mutual understanding. Then, as the scheme expanded and more tutors were needed, a strategy was devised to attract suitable individuals to take on the role. The new approach was to recruit teachers with particular orientations. It was preferred that they had some senior management responsibility to ensure that they could mobilize support for the project within the school, they were registered with the HEI for a part-time M.Phil or Ph.D. to ensure a thorough engagement with scholastic activity and their schools were to be paid a fee to allow for the allocation of additional non-contact time so that they had the time to take a share of the planning, preparation and administrative dimensions of the scheme. This strategy was applied in all its particulars in only one case although it was influential in other cases.

Establishing a Reflective Action Planning Group

Once there is an outline agreement to form a RAP group within a school, the partners must consider the question of recruitment. The following strategies could be considered:

Recruitment strategies

1   The tutor and in-school co-ordinator should produce a brief leaflet for distribution to all members of staff. It should make it clear that the programme provides opportunities for participants to engage in:

    • systematic school development work;
    • the pursuit of further academic awards through the submission of portfolios;
    • participation in group sessions at the end of the teaching day.

The leaflet should then invite members of staff to attend a presentation about the proposed programme.

2   The tutor and in-school co-ordinator should plan a detailed presentation to an invited audience using the diagram (Figure 3.1) to explain and discuss the model.

3   The head or another senior member of staff could have individual conversations with colleagues who might benefit from such a programme although there is a danger here that members of staff may feel pressured into joining only to withdraw at a later date.

If there are not enough volunteers to constitute a viable group, the school may wish to consider inviting colleagues from other schools to participate. This may be seen as a purely commercial enterprise designed to spread the cost of resourcing the group or it may be seen more positively as a means to foster collaboration with other schools. This happens typically when a secondary school wishes to build collaborative relationships with its feeder primary schools.

Once viability is assured, the tutor and the in-school co-ordinator must devise a programme and consult with the participants about its content.

The Programme

The programme should include sessions which are sufficiently regular and rich in terms of variety of input. The extent of the programme will be limited not only by the available budget but also by the amount of time that participants are able to devote to the programme. Our research and experience suggests that a successful group might have the characteristics set out below in Figure 3.2 although it is recognized that the model can operate successfully within a variety of different structures and settings.

Domestic Arrangements

The vast majority of teachers are discouraged from participating in award-bearing programmes because of the massive inconvenience of travelling to the HEI site at unsociable times of the day, and, since the whole purpose of this approach is to support teachers' contributions to school improvement, it is essential that the programme operates on the school site. However, it is important to create an ambience which is conducive to reflection and discussion by providing refreshments, a good-sized room, pleasantly decorated and comfortably furnished, and the usual audio-visual equipment.

Individual Tutorials

It is very important that each participant has regular tutorial support on an individual basis at least twice per term, which is usually arranged on the school site. This may be best provided by the tutor who is external to the

Figure 3.2

Typical Features of a RAP Programme

- 12–15 'twilight' sessions (4.00–6.00 p.m.) per year;
- a group of between 10 and 15 participants;
- the sessions led jointly by the in-school co-ordinator and the tutor;
- occasional guest speakers (teachers from other schools are favoured) and leadership of sections of the programme by members of the group (in well established groups);
- a balance between workshops to support the process, and seminars about substantive themes or issues;
- seminars in which participants make presentations about their work and the tutor prepares additional material to widen the debate;
- regular opportunities for participants to share experience of managing change and conducting inquiry.

---

school but it is quite possible that the in-school co-ordinator may be appointed by the HEI as an associate tutor and can provide tutorial support. Our experience tells us that the best way to arrange tutorials is for the school to provide a supply teacher who can release participants one at a time for their tutorials.

Access to Literature

Reading is essential to develop rigour. This is not just because of the award-bearing dimension but because effective school improvement depends on clarity and coherence of thinking, the validity of conclusions drawn from data, the availability of fresh ideas and the findings of research and inspection. Most schools have some kind of staff library, but these are rarely adequate to sustain a programme of this kind. The HEI has the responsibility therefore to ensure that participants have adequate access to literature. How can this be achieved when the programme is based in the school which may be a considerable distance from the university library? There are a number of strategies that can help to compensate for the lack of easy and regular access to a good educational library, as shown in Figure 3.3.

Of course there is no real substitute for using the library on a regular basis, but we are confident that the problem of access to literature can be significantly ameliorated if not completely overcome especially as individuals become familiar with the new computer-based technology.

Figure 3.3

Strategies for Accessing Literature

1   *The 'book box'*. University libraries are sometimes willing to let a tutor take a collection of the most commonly requested books to the school for teachers to borrow. This strategy does demand fastidious record keeping, however.

2   *Flexible regulations*. Universities committed to distance learning tend to have special regulations for distance learning students which enable them to keep books for longer periods and renew their loans through e-mail or by telephone

3   *The group library visit*. It is usually possible to use the school mini-bus to take a RAP group to the HEI library for a twilight session or even an additional Saturday morning session. If carefully managed in collaboration with the library staff, these sessions can at least establish the basic searching skills which can be used subsequently when participants visit on an individual basis.

4   *Remote searching through the Internet*. Most university libraries allow access to their catalogues through a website. Participants should therefore be able to log on at school or from their PC at home and conduct a search. Books identified in this way can always be purchased through mail order or secured through the inter-library loan system.

5   *Downloading material from the Internet*. An increasingly wide range of material is available from websites. The TES has an archive of articles going back over the past few years, and these can easily be located and copied on to a PC. Similarly, inspection reports and guidance material of all sorts are available through DfEE sponsored websites such as the 'Standards Site'. In addition, many university Schools of Education now have websites to which are attached papers written by their academic staff.

6   *Personal library visits during school holidays*. As participants become more familiar with the library and increasingly convinced of the value of library searching, they tend to want to make the journey during half-term breaks and the like. The motivation to do this will depend on the effectiveness of the other strategies mentioned above.

7   *Mutual support through web-based conferencing*. Participants can share their own reviews of books and articles and post these on the group's webpage. They can also list the resources they are able to share on a personal basis.

Working Within Ethical Boundaries

A RAP group should be engaging in a discourse which is both critical and authentic. Discussion within the support group is therefore likely to include sensitive issues and information about practice which affects colleagues who are not members of the group. High-quality discussion is also likely to include personal disclosures which participants would not necessarily wish to share beyond the confines of the support group. If individuals were to feel constrained by the lack of confidentiality, the discussion would be stilted and without genuine engagement with the issues.

Ethical principles for the programme should be agreed between its members at the start of the process and with the senior management of the school. Participants should also be urged to consider the ethical implications of their particular inquiry strategies and to respect the needs of their colleagues and their students. Figure 3.4 gives guidelines which are recommended as a basis for discussion in order to establish agreed principles for the group.

Figure 3.4

Ethical Guidelines for a RAP Group

1   Discussion which takes place in the group and in tutorials must be regarded as absolutely confidential.
2   It is unethical for any individual to make use of disclosures made within the group in other decision-making contexts.
3   Each individual's portfolio should be regarded as their own property and should be used entirely at their own discretion.
4   While group members are asked to produce appropriate papers for professional audiences at regular intervals, they should not be obliged to present all their papers to audiences within the school.
5   In the writing of evaluative material, group members should avoid identifying individual colleagues or students who might feature in the data.
6   Where individuals can be identified because of the context, the writer should always seek the agreement of those identified, firstly as to the validity of the data and secondly as to whether the material may be published.
7   Group members should have the right to develop a critical analysis of current practices and policies without fear of damage to their standing in the school.

(Frost, 1997: 59)

The Potential Role of RAP in School Improvement

In adopting the model and establishing a reflective action planning group, schools demonstrate commitment to the expectation that individual teachers will contribute to school improvement, and that there will also be impact on the school as a whole as a result of the presence and activities of the group. The nature of the impact depends largely on the extent to which the model is taken on by the school as a whole; the extent to which the RAP group is seen as complementary to other institutional groups and structures, acting as a focus for professional discourse, a source of support for individuals' 'change agentry' and a forum for the generation and discussion of ideas and strategies for school improvement.

Active involvement in an award-bearing programme is obviously not for every member of staff; indeed, the success of the school-based groups rests on the voluntary nature of the participation and on teachers identifying a developmental agenda which arises from their personal professional commitments and concerns. It is intended to be presented as an opportunity: it cannot be imposed. However, there are ways in which the presence of a group can provide the school with a focus for developmental activity and educational debate. The extent to which this is realized depends on how the programme is embraced by the school as a vehicle for school improvement and support for teacher-led change as opposed to a means for individual professional development; this in turn depends largely on the way in which the partnership between the school and the HEI is originally established and subsequently understood and managed. All RAP groups have a certain amount of impact in terms of raising the level of dialogue within the school as the teachers involved take their ideas, data analysis and proposals back into their departments and their own circles of contact amongst colleagues. Some schools have explored ways of extending this climate of critical discourse, for example by opening up some of the sessions with input on current educational issues to a wider group of staff and by inviting group members to lead INSET for their colleagues. The most highly developed use of the model involves an interactive relationship between the RAP group and the school development process; here, the group is used as a forum for the generation and discussion of ideas which are fed into the planning process. The group is also used to subject ideas emanating from other groups in the school to critical scrutiny. The model has also been used by other evaluation and development groups within the school, for example, those linked to aspects of the curriculum (see Chapter 5).

Clearly the in-school co-ordinator and either the head or an influential senior manager have crucial roles in recognizing the potential for the model and having the vision to use the group flexibly. The initiative for extending the influence of the group can come from its members or from the senior management team and/or the head, and is usually negotiated through the in-school co-ordinator to ensure that the character and ethos of the group is preserved or developed appropriately (for example, with regard to its ethical issues and principles).

At the same time, it is important to maintain the profile and status of the group within the school. Its participants need to be supported, actively and visibly, so that individual change agentry is allowed to flourish rather than be stifled through closed management structures or an apparent lack of interest. This demands a 'lightness of touch' on the part of the school management to enable teachers to pursue their own agendas and trust them to take responsibility for negotiating development priorities in line with those of the school, while at the same time recognizing the central contribution they are making, individually and collectively, to school improvement. Regular dialogue between school and HEI should underpin the programme so that the fundamental principles of partnership, school improvement and critical discourse are continually re-emphasized and the dynamics of the reflective action planning approach are reviewed and maintained, or adjusted in response to the changing context of the school's overall development process.

4 Reflective Action Planning

A Model for Teacher-Led School Improvement

As we suggested earlier in Chapter 3, it is helpful to break the reflective action planning model into its different constituents so as to consider the nature and role of each. A detailed explanation of the process, together with accompanying workshop guides and other materials has been set out in a previous publication (Frost, 1997) but, in the period since that guide was published, the model has been developed. Here, we give a summary of each part of the process and illustrate where appropriate with facsimiles based on the work of teachers who have used the model in the past.

Stage 1: Personal Vision-Building

This first stage of the process assumes that individual teachers need to develop greater clarity about ways in which they can contribute to school improvement; they need to develop the confidence and conviction to be able to enter into consultation about priorities and negotiation with colleagues, some of whom may have considerably more power and authority within the school. Teachers' transformative capacity, their capacity 'to make a difference', their 'agency' (Giddens, 1984) can be developed by helping them to become clearer about their values and interests, and therefore, their own concerns and priorities.

There are two stages to this part of the process:

(a) a workshop to explore the roots of individuals' professional concerns;
(b) the writing of an 'Initial Statement' to support a private reflection.

The workshop: at the very beginning of the programme the group leaders should arrange an activity in which participants work in pairs or trios to talk through their past experience, their roles of reponsibility, their professional values and so on. A series of headings such as those set out below could be provided with spaces for notes. It works well when A asks B about each heading and writes down the responses in the spaces provided. At the conclusion of the workshop, A and B can exchange their notes which can be taken away and used as an aid to further reflection (see Figure 4.1).

Figure 4.1

Possible Headings for Reflection

1   Professional history
2   Role/development last year
3   Issues arising from last year
4   The School Development Plan
5   Role this year
6   Strengths and needs
7   Values and interests
8   Consultation

Writing the initial statement: it is important to build on the workshop by asking participants to clarify their 'personal vision' in writing. This should not be a public document shared with senior managers or other colleagues unless the writer chooses to do so; rather it should be a private reflection which helps the individual to think it through. The group leaders should ask for these statements to be handed in so that they can make a critical response.

By providing a framework for 'personal vision building' we can strengthen the participants' capacity to play a fuller part in the professional discourse that shapes practice in their school. The activity strengthens the teachers' bargaining position as they enter into negotiation with their senior colleagues about priorities for development.

Stage 2: Personal Development Planning

Having clarified and strengthened their own view of what needs to be done to improve the school, individuals should then be asked to enter into a process of consultation and negotiation by producing a Personal Development Plan (PDP). Again, it is important for the teacher to be explicit and precise about their priorities, partly because their detailed planning will be more effective if it is based on a very precise articulation of the priorities or foci for development, but also because, in sharing the PDP with colleagues, the individual is in a sense seeking a mandate for action and so must be wary of misleading anyone about the nature of the development work intended.

Prospective change agents should be prepared to fight their corner when negotiating the content of their PDP but equally they should also be prepared to listen to those who may have a different, perhaps broader, view of the development priorities of the school as a whole. Personal priorities may well match closely the priorities set out in the school development plan, but it may be that adjustments have to be made in the light of colleagues' views about competing priorities or constraints such as the lack of funding. Alternatively a PDP might support an argument that the school development plan should be adjusted to accommodate new ideas. The important thing is to secure the support of senior managers and reach an understanding about goals which are realistic. Recent research in the school improvement field indicates that some foci are more fruitful than others, and that overload and multiple initiatives constitute obstacles to effective improvement processes (Gray et al., 1999) so it is the responsibility of senior managers to ensure that the proposed development work is likely to have a good 'effect size' and that, if necessary, the change agent is protected from their own enthusiasm.

Writing a Personal Development Plan: it is important that the PDP is seen as a public document, one which might be discussed with the headteacher and other stakeholders. It should be written in clear and precise language and be very brief (no more than a side of A4). It should include a rationale and a clear statement of perceived priorities. There is a good example of such a document in Chapter 7. Group leaders may wish to provide indicative headings and prompts but we suggest that the format is very simple.

Stage 3: Strategic Action Planning

An Action Plan sets out the detailed steps the change agent intends to take to address a specific development priority over a short time scale. The act of setting out intentions in the form of a written document which is made public within the school, demands that participants think through all stages of the process, and make a firm commitment to action. A good action plan will summarize the focus for development, and then set out the imagined series of events and activities which the change agent believes will result in improvement of some sort.

Where an individual has identified several development priorities in their PDP they will need to write an action plan for each one. The act of setting out all the tasks which have to be carried out may well serve to cause the change agent to reconsider the wisdom of taking on such a burden.

Format for an Action Plan: an Action Plan is a document intended to be made public within the school so, like the PDP, it needs to be written in a concise and accurate style which colleagues can read easily. Typical headings for an Action Plan might include the following (see Figure 4.2), but the plan may take a different form altogether, depending on the nature of the development work in hand.

Figure 4.2

Format for an Action Plan

Focus for development
The development priority or aspect of it and the context.

Inquiry strategies
The questions, the evidence needed, the data gathering techniques and so on.

Proposals for change
New practices, implementation, intended outcomes.

Targets and time scales
What and by when?

Reporting/dissemination
In what form, to whom, when?

Review
With whom, when?

The format offered here is not to be followed slavishly but used as a guide. In reality, individuals must structure the plan according to the nature of the project. The example below demonstrates how one individual has used the guide to develop her own plan (see Figure 4.3).

Figure 4.3

Facsimile of an Action Plan

Action Plan, First draft

Development Priority

In order to raise standards of achievement, I propose to develop an approach to the monitoring of student progress and the setting of targets for individual students.

Consultation

In the first instance I need to talk to my colleagues on the SMT: Derek about assessment, Annabel about the Curriculum and Malcolm about Staff Development. I shall arrange to have conversations with each on an individual basis.

Issues

The questions I need to explore are:

1 In what way can target setting and monitoring contribute to the raising of standards?
2 What kind of approach would be sufficiently rigorous and acceptable to my colleagues?
3 Who should be responsible for setting targets – HODs, subject teachers, pastoral tutors?
4 When and how often is it to be done?
5 How can we measure the effectiveness of the system?

Possible Strategies

First I need to conduct a basic reconnaissance to gather information about monitoring and target setting systems. This could include the following:

1 Set up working party including representatives of HODs, heads of year, SENCO, form tutors and subject teachers to look at target setting and monitoring.
2 Attend a short course on target setting (already arranged as part of our pastoral series).
3 Talk with Head of 6th Form about her experience of monitoring in Year 12.
4 Interview a group (4/5) of Year 7 students about their experience of target setting in the Primary school.
5 Visit the Queens School in Lincolnshire where OFSTED inspectors tell us there is good practice in this field.
6 Visit St Francis of Assisi School, Wood Green following their whole school INSET run by Haringey on target setting and monitoring.
7 Attend the DfEE/NFER conference on School Improvement.
8 Correspond through e-mail with a number of schools identified through the London School Improvement Network.

9   Visit the library at the June CANTARNET conference to gather literature about the topic.

Proposals for Change

It seems sensible to begin with Year 7. We should aim to ensure that every
Year 7 student is set targets which are specific, realistic and challenging and
that these targets are reviewed regularly. Details of who will do what, how
the targets will be agreed and when this will take place, will be proposed
after the second meeting of the working party in July.

Time Scale

We are under pressure from OFSTED to produce proposals for action on
target setting within the 40 day limit for Action Plans. I would like to set
up a pilot scheme with Year 7 in September 1997, which will be reviewed
and evaluated in the Summer term of 1998. The results of this review will
be passed back to SMT with a proposal, if successful, to extend the scheme
to other Year groups. I shall draft an action plan for this pilot after the first
meeting of the working party (June) and finalize it at the second meeting
in July.

Evidence for my portfolio

(a) Minutes of the working party.
(b) Summary of points from the Year 7 interviews.
(c) Reports on the 2 conferences and the 2 school visits.

It should be stressed that the Action Plan is a working document which
will need to be redrafted from time to time, in response to changing circumstances and in the light of experience of the development work.

Stage 4: Development Work

Clearly this part of the process is the major part; it is the whole point of the
exercise and so each of the following dimensions – collaboration, systematic
inquiry, changing practice, professional learning, and documenting the process
– are dealt with in turn. However, it is important to regard them as all part of
an integrated whole.

Consultation and Collaboration

This is a continuous thread running throughout the process. It begins with discussion about the individual's PDP through which the change agent seeks the agreement of colleagues and the authority to act. Subsequent action plans should be negotiated with key colleagues to ensure maximum commitment and support. Action plans themselves should specify the stakeholders who need to be consulted, the individuals and groups with whom it would be wise to collaborate and the responses and perceptions which might constitute part of the data to be collected.

Central to the reflective action planning approach to school improvement is the notion that there should be a very direct link between the individual teacher's personal development plan and the development priorities of the school or organization or corporate body. Emphasis on the role of reflection and personal development planning makes clear that the model is individual-centred. However, it has to be recognized that individual teachers work in organizations and belong to a wider professional community and, to that extent, their development work and their professional learning can only make sense in relation to the goals of the organization in which they work and the aims of the profession as a whole. This means that it is essential that the individual consults with appropriate colleagues because the outcomes of personal development planning and action planning are likely to be substantial changes in practice or the carrying out of inquiry/development work which is likely to affect a wide range of colleagues and students.

It is important to determine at the start of the process who should be consulted about the development work. In some schools there may be a 'line management' system where each member of staff has a designated person with whom they automatically consult. Where this is not the case, it is important to consider colleagues' management responsibilities and vested interests to ensure that there is sufficient consultation before embarking on any significant development work.

It is important to avoid any misunderstanding about the nature of consultation with the HEI tutor, which runs alongside the consultation within the school. The tutor cannot make judgements about whether particular views of the priorities for development are valid; this is a matter for negotiation between the change agents and their colleagues in the school. The tutor should be consulted for advice over such matters as inquiry methods, the issues arising, ways of presenting evidence and so on.

Anyone planning to take action to address an agreed development priority must recognize that they are accountable to their colleagues and have an obligation to report the outcomes to appropriate audiences within the school or organization. Reporting must not be seen merely as some kind of 'tokenistic' feedback, but as an essential part of the process of ongoing consultation with colleagues and other stakeholders in the school and, perhaps, within the wider community.

Systematic Inquiry

The RAP model assumes that effective school improvement is inquiry-based. There are two parts to the rationale: first we suggest that proposals for change need to be based on evidence which is seen to be valid by the majority of colleagues in the school; second, we suggest that the process of inquiry is seen as a vehicle for managing change. It has the potential to empower people by enabling voices to be heard, perspectives to be articulated and proposals to be debated. Not only does inquiry provide sound evidence to underpin particular initiatives, but it also develops the organizational culture of the school.

There is much to be learned from reading about and discussing various research traditions and paradigms, but much of the literature on research methodology is written by academics or professional researchers with an audience of other researchers in mind. Within RAP groups, the emphasis has to be on practicality and group leaders need to provide guidance which helps teachers to integrate inquiry into their professional lives. The following list of points has been developed through work with RAP groups (see Figure 4.4).

Figure 4.4

Practical Inquiry for School Improvement

1 Plan Inquiry Tasks that are 'Fit-For-Purpose'

Some school improvement work has suffered because teachers have been misled by the pseudo-scientific 'received wisdom' which often leads to dependence on surveys. So, we need to:

- be clear about the purpose of the inquiry, your aims, and the kind of evidence you really need;
- conduct an initial reconnaissance (gather the facts and analyse the situation);
- devise inquiry strategies which match your actual purpose – distinguish, for example, between the need for numbers and the need for insights;
- pilot your strategies and instruments (for example, an interview schedule) and remove the glitches.

2 Use Efficient, Institution-Friendly Inquiry Strategies

Time is a scarce commodity in schools and we cannot afford to let 'research' get in the way of the main professional activity of teaching. To develop the transformational capacity of the school, we need to cultivate collaboration through inquiry. So, we need to:

- make a realistic assessment of the availability of time and plan accordingly, avoid disrupting teaching;
- consider the ethical issues but do not avoid conflict;
- integrate data gathering into teaching or other professional activity;
- recognize and make full use of data which already exists;
- borrow and adapt devices/instruments designed and used by others;
- choose straightforward strategies which colleagues will be able to understand and use;
- choose strategies which result in data which are easy to analyse.

3 Integrate Inquiry into a Managed Change Process

Often a school improvement initiative flounders because those responsible for leading the change have neglected to think about the process as a whole. It is important to plan strategically. So, we need to:

- draw colleagues and students into the inquiry activity;
- plan for the analysis, interpretation and validation of data;
- plan for engagement with the school as an organization; consider reporting, disseminating, presenting, reflecting, debating, influencing policy making;
- anticipate and bid in advance for resources for appropriate staff development events;
- choose strategies which raise awareness, get people talking and maximize involvement;
- gather data about the change process itself to maximize personal and organizational learning.

It is often the case that practitioner research tends to draw on a limited repertoire of inquiry methods, typically the survey. This approach is based on a received wisdom about objectivity and sampling which is rarely helpful in the teacher–led school improvement scenario. More recently of course, the availability of student performance data tends to give further credence to the idea that statistical analysis is the most valid form of inquiry. There is clearly a role for such quantitative work particularly inasmuch as we need to be able to pinpoint underachieving categories or engage in benchmarking exercises. However, RAP group leaders need to open up discussion about possible sources of data and evidence gathering procedures, particularly of the qualitative sort. The list below could be helpful in such a discussion (see Figure 4.5).

Figure 4.5

What Inquiry Includes

- reading
- reflecting
- visiting/observing
- evidence analysis
- evidence gathering
- conversation
- writing

This overhead transparency has been used to help participants develop a broader view of inquiry. It highlights the role of common sense investigative strategies such as visiting other schools, perhaps Beacon Schools and having conversations with key individuals. It also distinguishes the analysis of evidence that is already available from the evidence that has to be gathered deliberately. The overhead transparency in Figure 4.6 below has been used to help explore some of the data that already exists in the 'data rich environment' of the modern school.

Figure 4.6

Data That Already Exists

1 Pupil assessment data
2 Comparative pupil performance data
3 Pupil records
4 Pupils' work
5 Home school correspondence
6 Procedural documentation
7 Development planning documentation
8 Curriculum/teaching documentation
9 Inspection reports
10 Data from previous inquiry

Clearly there is likely to be a need for data that does not already exist, and so participants will need to consider data gathering strategies, but as indicated earlier, these need to be chosen carefully to ensure that they yield the maximum information for the minimum input in terms of time and effort.

The handout in Figure 4.7 below has been used to help explore a wide range of data gathering strategies.

Figure 4.7

Evidence to be Gathered

1   Observation of Lessons by Colleagues

Most people feel a bit vulnerable when being observed and so it is important for the observer and the observed to agree on what will be observed and how feedback will be given and recorded.

2   A Classroom Journal / Research Diary

The teacher's own observations and reflections can be recorded during the lesson or immediately afterwards. These notes could be structured in advance or just a matter of whatever appears to be significant or interesting.

3   Tape recordings

Both video and audio recordings can be useful in recalling events for later discussion. They can be expensive and technically demanding if the aim is more sophisticated than this.

4   The Change Agent's Journal / Research Diary

The teacher who is managing a change process can record critical incidents, issues and feelings as they arise. These can then be recalled in order to reflect on progress and to reshape an action plan.

5   Students' Journals

Students' perceptions can be gathered routinely by asking the class, or perhaps just a small sample of students, to record their thoughts and feelings about the lesson in a notebook. This is probably best structured in advance by providing headings and particular time slots for journal entries to be made.

6   Interviews with Students

It is best to choose a sample of 'reliable informants' and ask someone (a student teacher, a Classroom Assistant, a colleague) to conduct a semi-structured interview. Tell the interviewer what you think the issues might be, but make sure the students have the space to raise their own. It is often more productive to interview students in groups of 3–5.

7   Interviews with Teachers

Again, semi-structured or conversational interviews are best, and the issues can easily be noted down. Make sure that everybody knows the ground rules about who can see the notes and so on.

8   Ephemeral Artefacts

There may be such things as notes on flip charts following a team brain-storming session or a classroom activity. There may be vital evidence here which can be extracted and used to inform subsequent analysis.

9   Students' Work

Clearly this represents a substantial body of evidence which can be analysed systematically to generate insights about students' learning. It is a potentially efficient form of inquiry in that teachers already have an obligation to mark the work and therefore carrying out other analytical tasks alongside the marking would not consume much additional time.

10   Students' Reflections Within Homework

Students can be asked to make comments about what they think they have learnt and what they think about the activities and materials used in the lessons, as part of their written follow up tasks.

11   Teachers' Responses to Students' Work

Teachers' annotations and comments on students' work, particularly when they identify what has been learnt and what has yet to be learnt, can be an excellent source of evidence on students' learning.

12 Photographs

These are particularly useful in the classroom or other social settings such as the playground or the canteen. They can be used to recall activities and to stimulate discussion with students and others about the events represented by the snapshots.

13 Surveys

These are the last in the list because they tend to be over-used. They can be very inefficient, involving a great deal of work for little reward in terms of the quality of the data gathered. To be productive, they need to be carefully designed and piloted. However, having said that, sometimes they can be an efficient way of producing data particularly if it is important to know something about a large population.

There is a limit to the amount of guidance that can be given at the start of the process. Our experience tells us that it is better to ensure that there are sufficient opportunities for participants to try out their plans on a variety of critical friends but most crucially the RAP group as a whole. The group should be an effective forum for debate about the appropriateness of individuals' plans for inquiry-based development work.

Changing Practice

The early stages of the RAP process address the need to enhance the participants' agency and the need to identify development priorities that are in harmony with the school's development plans. Within the box marked 'development work', it is tempting to see the 'collaboration' and 'inquiry' as the means and 'changing practice' and 'professional learning' as the ends. We suggest that to see change as a matter of implementation is grossly inadequate; rather, we suggest that change must be seen as a complex and challenging process which can be supported through membership of the RAP group.

So how can a RAP group support the process of change initiated and sustained by individual teachers? The RAP group leaders need to be able to draw upon the management of change literature to help participants conceptualize the change process, but this is not necessarily best done in the context of a discrete seminar; ideas are often more meaningful when introduced as part of a response to issues arising out of participants' presentations about their own development work. However, there are some fundamental and recurring ideas that can be introduced early in the proceedings.

The idea of distributive leadership: one of the clear messages arising from studies of school effectiveness is that strong leadership is an important determining factor in school improvement (Sammons et al., 1995), but an emphasis on the role of the headteacher is unhelpful if it obscures what has been learnt about the positive benefits of shared leadership (see Mortimore et al., 1988; Angus, 1993). Fullan's account of 'change agentry' and the 'moral purpose' of education supports his claim that 'all teachers are change agents' (Fullan, 1993) and this is an important text in exploring the proposal that reflective action planners have first to accept the challenge to exercise leadership.

The idea that change challenges the self: again Fullan's work is invaluable in providing a rich account of the meaning of change for individuals (Fullan, 1991). The work of the change agent has to start from an understanding of the anxiety and sense of threat experienced by colleagues when they are confronted by the prospect of change. Change is not simply a rational process of implementing what is evidently a better practice than the one currently in place. Change challenges individuals' values and beliefs and threatens to 'de-skill' them.

The idea that the trajectory of change is unpredictable: Fullan's slogan, 'Change is a Journey, Not a Blueprint' is still useful for demystifying the idea of rational planning (Fullan, 1993). The whole idea of development planning and systematic planned change is beguiling and can lead to an unrealistic expectation that the process will unfold according to plan. Change agents can then experience negative emotions such as anxiety, disappointment and guilt when events fail to unfold in the way predicted. Since the publication of 'Change Forces' in 1993, Fullan has updated his account of the complexity of the process of change (Fullan, 1999), and it is this complexity that can be profitably explored through discussion in the RAP group sessions.

The idea that the implementation of new materials involves a change in pedagogy: the legacy of the 'research, development and diffusion' (RD & D) model was a deeply flawed expectation that, once the choice of curriculum materials or other educational practice had been made, implementation was a relatively simple matter. Within the RAP group, it is important to explore the way new practices demand a new approach to teaching and learning, and this may require classroom observation and other methods of investigation coupled with mentoring, coaching and other forms of support for professional development.

The idea that changes in teaching and learning involve new beliefs and values: there is a growing consensus that the key to school improvement is a focus on teaching and learning (Reynolds, 1999; Barber, 1999) but some are misguided in their belief that it is simply a rational process whereby we come to know 'what works' and then disseminate and implement better 'instructional practices'. There are of course issues to do with the level of skill with which a teacher uses a particular instructional approach but more fundamentally, there are values and beliefs that underpin teaching styles and these have to be articulated and reformulated in order to change teaching and learning approaches with any degree of success.

The idea that new practices may involve restructuring: one of the most compelling reasons for ensuring that senior management is involved in the establishment and maintenance of a RAP group is that some initiatives are likely to lead to proposals for changing the structures which help to shape educational practices (see Chapter 7 for example). There is a fundamental relationship between 'agency' and 'structure' (Giddens, 1984) in that individual teachers can exercise bottom-up power to change the structures that constrain and shape their practices. The scope of the discussion within RAP group sessions therefore has to include issues concerned with the school's organizational structures. Elliott (1993b, 1998a) provides an excellent explanation of the application of Giddens's theory to the management of change in schools.

The idea that school improvement necessarily involves cultural change: an important lesson learnt from the experience of the IQEA (Improving the Quality of Education for All) project is that 'school improvement works best when a clear and practical focus for development is linked to simultaneous work on the internal conditions within the school' (Hopkins et al., 1997). By 'internal conditions', they mean the dimensions of the school's capacity to handle change and improvement. RAP groups have used workshop materials based on typologies of school cultures to provide a framework for discussion and tools for analysis (see Frost, 1997). The essential point is that the dominant professional culture in the school or within a particular team strongly influences, if not actually determines, educational practice through the framework of beliefs, norms, values and procedures which constitute that culture. Change agents therefore need to explore strategies for developing cultures if their developmental goals are to be fully realized.

Clearly, all of the above is concerned with the process of change but RAP groups need also to consider outcomes; how these can be assessed, evaluated and demonstrated. There needs therefore to be some discussion about the potential impact of participants' initiatives, and ultimately some evaluation of development work which includes an assessment of the actual impact or at least those aspects which are assessable. These issues are discussed in greater depth in Chapter 10.

Professional Learning

As was made clear in Chapter 2, the RAP model represents an attempt to get away from an individualistic approach in which the main outcome is the rather loosely defined professional development of the participants. Nevertheless, we suggest that school improvement entails the professional development of both those participating directly and those involved in or affected by the participants' initiatives. However, as suggested in Chaper 2, we reject the idea of professional learning as training whereby something is done to teachers in order to secure the implementation of new practices. The change process is complex and involves professional learning on the part of all concerned.

From our interviews with participants and their senior managers we know that the RAP group plays an important role in helping participants reflect on their own learning as change agents. This learning needs to be made explicit and visible within group discussions so that participants can learn collectively from their combined experience. Leaders of RAP groups can determine the level of individual development according to the extent to which they can recognize the sorts of learning set out in Figure 4.8 below.

Figure 4.8

Participants' Professional Learning

1 Developing Agency

Participants develop their confidence and feelings of self-worth through developing their voice. They use the RAP group as a forum within which they can rehearse their articulation of their ideas. They become more skilled at presenting their ideas both verbally and in writing to a wider variety of audiences. They become more accustomed to argument.

2 Developing Understanding

Participants are able to explore what are sometimes new and often conceptually difficult areas. They are able to extend their vocabulary and to become more at ease with wide ranging analytical discussion of educational practice.

3 Clarifying Strategic Thinking

Participants are able to rehearse their strategic plans within group discussion and tutorial sessions and to develop their acumen as managers of change.

4 Improving Practice

Through systematic inquiry into their own teaching or other aspects of their professional role, participants are able to develop their 'mastery' (Fullan, 1993). This involves the development of practical skills as well as a rethink about the appropriateness of particular practices.

5 Acquiring New Knowledge

Through the wide ranging discussion, informed as it is by research and inspection findings, participants are able to become more familiar with developments in education. They become accustomed to reaching out beyond the confines of their subject to embrace more fundamental questions and engage in the wider discourse within the educational community as a whole.

6 Developing Self-Knowledge

Participants are drawn into a more reflexive mode of development in which they are called upon to reflect on their own practice and to become more aware of their own strengths and weaknesses.

Participants' action plans are likely to include the intention to organize some kind of staff development opportunity for their colleagues. The group sessions provide a good forum within which participants can explore the concept of professional development and can evaluate a range of teacher-led strategies. Questions for consideration include those set out in Figure 4.9 below.

Figure 4.9

Professional Development Opportunities

- What funding is available and how does an individual bid for those funds to support a staff development opportunity?
- What is the most cost effective approach given the availability of funding?
- What expertise do we have within the school which could be shared?
- What factors determine the quality of a staff development experience?
- Is there a particular need to go off-site and if so, where would be most conducive and what would it cost?
- How can time be used most cost effectively taking into account colleagues' energy levels?
- What kind of activities are most likely to lead to maximum involvement of colleagues and their fullest commitment to subsequent new practices?

There will be occasions when external expertise is needed but change agents need to have a clear understanding with the provider about the nature of the need and how this will be met. The recent publication of the 'Standards' for Qualified Teachers, SENCOs and Subject Leaders provides a helpful set of checklists against which individuals can begin to assess their own competence and participants may well find these useful in designing an audit of staff development needs for example (TTA, 1998).

Documenting the Process

We tend to think of learning as being something which happens to individuals but there is a sense in which we can talk of 'organizational learning' (Senge, 1990; Argyris and Schon, 1996). We would not want to be too anthropomorphic about this – organizations are not organisms – but it is possible to think of the way in which a school can become increasingly cohesive and develop a strong 'collective vision'. However, this is very difficult to do unless the institutional memory is nourished in a deliberate way. We may all know of examples of innovations that have had considerable impact for a short period of time, and, as key individuals either leave the school or become focused on other priorities, they have simply been abandoned and eventually forgotten about. Within the RAP model, we are interested in long-term school improvement and so a key part of the process of change is the documentation of the process. According to the Business Archives Council, the idea of institutional archiving is well established in other organizational contexts and considered to be vital in order to be able to build on successes and learn from mistakes.

Stage 5: Portfolio Development

An academic award usually demands the submission of assessable assignments of one sort or another, but the traditional essay format can be an obstacle to the authentic pursuit of school improvement goals (see Chapter 2). We have found that the portfolio is a far more useful vehicle for the documentation of teachers' development work. The word 'portfolio' suggests a collection of separate items of evidence which would have been produced in the first instance for a variety of audiences and for a variety of purposes. For example, the *audience* for an action plan would have been the writer's colleagues and other stakeholders; its *purpose* would have been consultation and negotiation.

In order to preserve the evidence of the development work, a reflective action planner would simply collect any item of evidence and store it in a ring binder or something similar. By evidence, we mean artefacts or real documents which have been produced for professional purposes and for professional audiences. This collection is likely to include the sort of items of evidence illustrated by the list in Figure 4.10 below.

Figure 4.10

Evidence for the Portfolio: Some Examples

- a Personal Development Plan;
- an interview schedule;
- an OHT used in a presentation to a staff meeting;
- a discussion paper written for a department meeting;
- a letter sent to parents explaining the introduction of a new target-setting system;
- a budget for a proposed resources centre;
- a memo from the Headteacher suggesting changes to a first draft of an action plan.

Such a collection does not of itself constitute a portfolio; it will lack coherence and will not be intelligible to someone who is not familiar with the events and the context. In order to create a portfolio, the individual has to organize and present the material and the way this is done will depend on the purpose of the portfolio. Some possible purposes are outlined in Figure 4. 11 below.

Figure 4.11

Purposes of a Portfolio

- as a private record of events to aid reflection and planning;
- as a tool used within a formal appraisal context;
- as a basis for a review of progress (of a particular initiative) with an LEA advisor, a senior manager, colleague or other critical friend;
- as a summative record of achievement used to support an application for a new post;
- as a submission for the purposes of accreditation.

The particular design of the portfolio – the way it is constructed and organized – will be determined in part by the individual writer's creativity and in part by the particular purpose the writer has in mind, but there are some basic principles which tend to apply whatever the case.

Figure 4.12

Basic Principles for Portfolio Construction

1 Select the Evidence

All of the documentation arising from a school improvement initiative may be so voluminous as to be inaccessible to anyone other than the individual who led the initiative. Some of it may be insignificant or repetitive. The author needs therefore to make a careful selection from the evidence. This corresponds to the editing process involved in constructing a 'case record' within a research context (Stenhouse, 1978; Rudduck, 1985).

2 Order the Evidence

The most obvious way to do this is chronologically so that the reader follows a narrative which spans a period of time. There may be alternatives however, for example, where the portfolio is organized according to themes or strands.

3 Label the Evidence

Each item of evidence must be labelled in such a way that it can easily be referred to. It is inappropriate to use page numbers that run throughout as in a dissertation or paper so some kind of coding system is required so that each item can be identified in a list of contents.

4 Add Explanatory Commentary

Items of evidence alone will not be intelligible unless they are accompanied by commentary which puts the evidence in context, explains its origin in terms of audience and purpose and provides some rationale for the inclusion of the evidence in the portfolio.

5 Add a Critical Narrative

This is both an interpretation and an analysis written in narrative form. A critical narrative is essential when the portfolio is being submitted for accreditation but we suggest that it is essential whatever the purpose. It is a first person 'story' in which the author draws upon both the available literature and the evidence included in the portfolio to account for the process of their development work and to engage in a critical discussion about issues arising.

6 Bind the Portfolio

It is clearly important to preserve the order of the documents presented in the portfolio so it is vital that it is bound in such a way that it does not disintegrate in transit. In our experience, spiral binding is successful in that it allows for easy turning of the pages while preserving the structure and integrity of the document.

So portfolios should include *evidence*, *commentary* and *critical narrative*, and it is the careful and deliberate compilation of these elements that make the portfolio coherent and intelligible to the external reader.

Stage 6: Review

If 'change is a journey, not a blueprint' (Fullan, 1993) then it is important to build into the development process opportunities to join with colleagues in taking stock of progress and to review the unfolding change process from different perspectives. Whatever targets and goals were agreed at the outset may have become redundant or may need adjusting. Thus development planning is an organic process rather than existing as an inert document handed down from above.

This 'stock-taking' dialogue can also present a good forum for the recognition of the individual teacher's achievement and a realistic assessment of the viability of a particular development. This can lead to career development or to the allocation of appropriate resources. At the very least the review process should identify fresh targets which are realistic and adjusted in the light of experience.

It is important from the outset to clarify what mechanisms exist for the individual teacher to engage with the school as an organization. This process should be part of the contract with the school. There may be a line management system with clear lines of accountability and review. On the other hand, there may be more freedom to establish other relationships based on critical friendship or mentoring. The development work may be discussed as an integral part of the appraisal system. Whatever the case, it is important to ensure not only ongoing professional consultation but also a summative review of what has been achieved in order that fresh targets can be set and the teacher's work can be given full recognition within the school (see Figure 4.13).

Figure 4.13

Some Questions to Guide the Review Process

What were the original development priorities?
What action plans were agreed at the outset?
In what ways were action plans amended along the way?
Were there any success criteria built into the action plans?
What insights emerged from inquiry?
To what extent were the action plans carried out?
What obstacles were experienced?
What has been the impact of the development work so far?
To what extent have any success criteria been met?
What lessons have been learnt by yourself?
What are the implications for the school's structures and procedures?
What are the implications for future development priorities?

Stage 7: Accreditation

We take the term 'accreditation' to mean the process whereby credit towards a further academic award is earned for the acquisition of professional knowledge in a professional context. It may well be possible to use the RAP model without the award-bearing dimension, but we suggest that accreditation has a number of clear advantages. It draws in expertise from higher education and subsidizes academics' involvement through the DfEE's funding for CPD; it enhances the development work through the rigour demanded by academic assessment criteria; it enriches the development work through the nature of academic discourse; and it provides a framework for reflection which otherwise would be difficult to foster as part of the busy life of schools and the pursuit of further academic awards is a source of motivation and pride for the participants.

A particular RAP programme needs to be based on a clear and firm shared understanding about the nature of the accreditation and the rules that govern its operation. The checklist in Figure 4.14 below can be used as an aid to planning.

Figure 4.14

Questions to Ask about Accreditation

1   What is the level of the award offered; masters? postgraduate? level 3?

2 What is the structure of the award, the number of credits per module and the routes of progression?
3 What are the assessment criteria for each module in the accreditation structure?
4 What are the requirements of the module in terms of the nature and extent of the work to be submitted?
5 What are the requirements of the award as a whole?
6 What are the regulations and conventions in respect of time scales and deadlines for submission of work?
7 What are the protocols for presentation, including such matters as how to make references and what to include in title pages?

The requirements of the module or unit of accreditation should be made clear in a handbook or similar guidance material provided by the HEI. It may be the case that the regulations of the accrediting body do not allow for the submission of a portfolio as the only item of 'coursework'. If this is the case it is possible to extract the critical narrative part of the portfolio and develop it into the more traditional essay or dissertation format which can be submitted along with the evidence in the form of a case record. This should not make any difference to the development work or to the use of the portfolio; it simply adds a further stage to the presentation. Similarly, the idea of a portfolio may present a challenge to the HEI's assessment criteria which may include, for example, a criterion which specifies a 'literature review'. Conversely, the criteria might not include an item such as 'appropriateness of inquiry strategies to the professional concern'. Where an award-bearing, teacher-led school improvement programme is being considered, the prospective partners may well want to consider whether the existing regulations and criteria are adequate for the purpose and whether there is scope for developing these. The current inspection of award-bearing CPD provision is focusing attention on the question of the impact of CPD programmes on students' learning, and this may well present a challenge where traditionally the assessment criteria have been concerned solely with the intellectual development of the individual rather than with school improvement or school development.

Stage 8: External Networking

There is a danger of insularity, complacency and self-satisfaction in any programme located in and centred on a single school. We need to look beyond the boundaries of our institutions to find the challenge and support which comes from interaction within wider networks. It is important therefore that those who are designing programmes to support reflective action planning should take steps to ensure that the critical discourse is extended in a number of ways.

Networking across schools: participants should be encouraged to engage with colleagues in other schools who might be engaged in similar or related development work. This can be facilitated by contributing to and by reading journals which carry reports of teachers' development work. Participants should also be encouraged to take advantage of conferences which are likely to provide contact with other teachers interested in school development or practitioner inquiry. Individual contacts can lead to visits to each other's schools and other peer learning projects, this being particularly effective in the context of a local or regional network where it can lead to more direct contact between colleagues. Chapter 9 explores the theme of professional networks in detail and offers a case study of Canterbury Action Research Network (CANTARNET) which has been established around the RAP groups within the Canterbury scheme and organizes conferences for teachers, publishes accounts of their work in its own journal, *The Enquirer*, and operates its own website (CANTARNET) through which an internet discussion forum facility is being developed.

Networking nationally and internationally: there are a number of different professional networks both within education and across the disciplines. The HEI tutor should be able to provide information about these so that teachers can engage with the discourse collectively and as individuals; this can be formalized through direct links with particular groups. The Internet provides opportunities for anyone to access and engage in the wider debate at their convenience.

Conclusion: The Central Role of Critical Reflection

Reflection is an integral part of the exercise of professional judgement. Teaching could hardly take place at all without the capacity for the minute-by-minute decision making that Schon (1983) called 'reflection in action'. However, more deliberate reflection is also essential in order to make sense of the complexity of the professional context and to develop a critical perspective on practice. School improvement therefore depends on sustained critical reflection. We suggest that the model offered here provides a secure framework for such critical reflection. It takes place on both an individual basis and collaboratively. The process of personal vision-building helps to strengthen the individual's resolve; the subsequent consultations and negotiation about development priorities and action plans draws the individual into layers of collaborative reflection. To take forward the development work itself the change agent creates many opportunities for collaborative reflection in the form of discussions and deliberations which arise in working groups, interviews, staff development events and so on. Ultimately, the aim is to enable the school to know itself better, to improve particular practices and to develop as an organization.

5 Reflections on Collaborative Inquiry

Following a presentation to the school's staff about the proposed pilot project, one of the more sceptical members of the audience asked if we were recommending the inquiry-based approach on the basis of any personal experience. The project leaders, David Frost and Jim Nixon, were able to say that, yes, they had experienced the benefits of self-critical inquiry at first hand and, furthermore, they were committed to continuing to use it to develop their practice as the tutors for the proposed group (this issue was explored more fully in Chapter 2).

The methods used to evaluate our practice as leaders of RAP groups and to develop the scheme as a whole were shaped by the values underpinning the scheme itself. It was felt that, if teachers were being asked to engage in self-critical inquiry, then the HEI tutor should do the same. We went along with Elliott (1993a), who argued that 'academics' who seek to facilitate teachers' action research and write about it have an obligation to undertake 'second-order action-research' in which they look critically at their own practice as teacher educators. This might help to avoid the misrepresentation of action research in a way which perpetuates and legitimates the hierarchical relations between academics and teachers. However, despite this earnest commitment at the pilot stage, it was difficult to sustain the research dimension when it relied upon the determination of just one or two individuals, so when the scheme was extended, David invited other RAP group leaders, amongst them the co-authors of this book, to join with him to establish a collaborative action research project (The ESACS Project) to evaluate and develop it. (ESACS is an acronym which stands for Evaluating a School-based Award-bearing Curriculum Development Scheme. The nature of the scheme has changed significantly since the beginning of the project, so the meaning of the title is less relevant than it was.)

In this chapter, we give an outline of the nature and process of our action research and explore the ways in which such an approach can improve professional practice and support change. We consider the issues which have emerged during the course of our collaboration and examine both the benefits and limitations of collaborative action research.

The Need for Collaboration

At the outset, we believed that the collaborative approach would provide moral support, sustain momentum, provide a vehicle for the management of the innovation and generate a critical perspective.

Collaboration as a source of moral support. This might be seen as self-indulgent, but it is a good way of beginning or sustaining action research where there are formidable constraints. The nature of our innovative scheme was known to threaten interests within the HEI which inevitably led to conflict. In such a situation, individuals draw heavily on collaboration, which 'strengthens resolve, permits vulnerability to be shared and carries people through those failures and frustrations that accompany change in its early stages' (Hargreaves, 1995: 151).

Collaboration to sustain momentum. As with the teachers involved in the scheme, we were also victims of conflicting priorities, competing agendas and the continual business and messiness of everyday professional activity. Collaborative research involved mutual expectations which helped us to transcend the vicissitudes of our professional and personal lives, which were sometimes overwhelming.

Collaboration as a vehicle for managing change. Collaborative action research offered an alternative to the training which was a central feature of the change strategy preferred by the senior managers of the HEI. The idea of training presupposes that we already know what 'best practice' looks like, but we were involved in an experimental innovation, so our involvement in dialogue based on shared experience and the analysis of data was a far more effective way to improve our practice and develop the school improvement scheme.

Collaboration to generate a critical perspective. As the project gathered momentum, we became increasingly aware of the power of our dialogue to enable us to engage in 'critical social science' (Carr and Kemmis, 1986) and challenge the 'conceptual and perceptual myopia' which can accompany the solitary enterprise (Bridges, 1996).

Collaboration and Ethics

It was clear from the outset that we needed to address concerns about the relationship between ourselves and others who had legitimate interests in our research, particularly since the research involved a number of schools in the same locality. We needed to protect those interests while at the same time allowing ourselves scope to address the issues arising from our research without undue constraints. Schools in Kent at the time were in fierce competition for 'customers', and headteachers were understandably sensitive about any information that might be disclosed about their schools. We wanted the heads to feel secure without giving them a veto. Similarly, we did not want the teachers involved to feel threatened by our data gathering, but we nevertheless wanted the freedom to discuss sensitive matters. At our early meetings, we discussed in detail 'the right to know versus the right of others to a degree of privacy' (Pring, 1984: 8).

More important perhaps was the fact that our commitment to partnership had implications for the composition and membership of the research team. We (Frost, Head, Durrant and Holden) were core activists wishing to research our own practice and evaluate the scheme, but there were different levels of participation beyond this. Each of the co-tutors in the five schools represented in the project became 'nominal members' or sleeping partners. This meant that, although they would normally not attend the research team meetings or be involved directly in any of the research activity, they nevertheless had the right to be kept informed of our proceedings through written accounts and to attend any of our meetings if they felt it necessary. This was doubly important because each school was asked to designate a named person whose responsibility it was to scrutinize our activity, keep the headteacher informed and, if necessary, intervene in the interests of the school. In some cases, this representative was one of the sleeping partners, which meant that the quality of the written accounts had to be sufficient to make them aware of the issues.

The Code of Practice, negotiated with the headteachers of the schools concerned, set out our research focus, and indicated the kind of data we would gather and the rules governing the data collection and subsequent reporting. An extract from that document is reproduced in Figure 5.1 below.

Figure 5.1

Extract from ESACS Project Code of Practice

Confidentiality

The research team makes a clear and firm commitment to the strictest confidentiality concerning the sharing of evidence from the schools taking part. The research team also makes a specific undertaking that data will not be disseminated beyond the confines of the team.

Methodological Ethics

1   All participants and other individuals affected will be asked for their permission for any evidence about their participation in the project to be used in the research.
2   Where evidence is gathered through observation, those observed will be invited to discuss and agree the accuracy and validity of the evidence.

3 Where evidence is gathered through interview, individuals will be invited to agree to the inclusion of the evidence gathered. Where an individual requests it, items will be deleted from transcripts.
4 No individual will be identified beyond the confines of the research team.
5 The critical narrative writing of individual participants will not be seen by anyone who is not that person's tutor or a tutor authorized to assess the work.
6 Records of tutorials will not be seen by anyone who is a colleague of the tutee.
7 All evidence gathering strategies and opportunities will be made known to all parties concerned and their agreement will be sought.
8 Previous research has shown the importance of biographical data in such studies but no teacher will be put under any pressure to divulge any personal information and such data would only be reported in a generalized and anonymous form.
9 Data about development work in the schools will only be gathered in as much as it impacts on the effectiveness of the scheme.

Reporting Ethics

1 Headteachers will have the right to see and discuss any case study reports prior to dissemination beyond the confines of the research team.
2 No reports will be released until all relevant parties (the headteachers and participating staff) have been consulted.
3 Reports will only report on issues in a general and anonymous form and all reasonable efforts will be made to ensure the anonymity of both schools and individual members of staff.

(Frost, 1995)

We hoped that these arrangements would ensure a high degree of ownership of the scheme and its evaluation.

Our Deliberative Process

The research and development process was driven by what became an intense critical conversation over a three-year period. This conversation was a key element in our methodology; it was the means by which we planned our data gathering, and it was also a process of analysis. Our core team meetings were held in the evenings at team members' houses and in pubs, and it was in these informal settings that we developed theories about our work as individual

RAP group leaders and made decisions about the development of the scheme as a whole. The informality of the setting was a conscious choice; some of us were full-time teachers, others had very full schedules and our research activities were on the margins of our professional lives, so daytime meetings were impossible. But the choice was also based on the realization that we would have to take deliberate steps to overcome the inhibitions which sprang from perceived differences of position and status. The ambience created by the kitchen table and the pub supper was a significant feature of our process as a research team and it helped us to overcome our inhibitions.

Perhaps all research teams have similar difficulties; in our case, we felt that the issues of position and status had to be confronted directly through a self-conscious exploration of our identities and perceptions of each other. At the first meeting the core team consisted of David Frost, a well-established academic from the HEI who had piloted the scheme and had devised the research project; Michael Head, who had retired the previous year as head-teacher of one of the project schools and had been recruited by David as a part-time tutor with the HEI; Gary Holden who was a senior teacher in another of the project schools, had been one of David's master's students and who was just about to become co-tutor of the RAP group newly established in his school; Rosanne Mullings, the only one of us with a Ph.D. at the time, who was a Head of Department in one of the project schools and co-tutor with Michael of the RAP group there; and Judy Durrant, a teacher who had left her post to start a family, and was at the time a member of one of the RAP groups.

There were obvious differences between us in terms of the kinds of expertise and the levels of confidence we brought to this joint enterprise. At our first meeting we explored the mutuality of our ideas, values and interests, and discovered a high level of consensus. We then went on to explore our aspirations and vested interests as individuals: for example, one of us had a professional obligation to produce publications to support the HEI's bid in the forthcoming 'research assessment exercise'; another of us was yet to complete her Masters degree and was keen to have a context for her own research; and so on. Like Waters-Adams (1994), we are convinced that a commitment to the collaborative approach has to be reconciled with the recognition of the role of individual motivation. He points to the dangers of entering into a collaborative process which may be a 'long and often painful development' (Waters-Adams, 1994: 208). Our experience was that it was indeed a long and challenging process, but the joys far outweighed the pain involved. Our collaboration was based on the happy coincidence of personal agendas as well as a set of shared beliefs.

The Focus of the Research and Data-Gathering Strategies

The issues that emerged from the pilot project were distilled into a set of thematic headings which were taken up by the ESACS group as starting points for discussion (see Figure 5.2 below).

Figure 5.2

The Themes Emerging from the Pilot

The nature of collaborative relationships
The management of development priorities
The nature of the tutor's role
The effectiveness of the support group
The benefits to the institution
The benefits to the individual participants
The nature of evidence and the process of accreditation
The organizational environment of the project

We concentrated on the five schools in which the tutors of the ESACS Project team were leading RAP groups, so that we were, in effect, conducting a multi-site case study. We used two parallel strategies for collecting evidence: one we described as 'routine data gathering', and the other as 'additional data gathering'.

Routine data gathering. Those of us who were tutors attached to RAP groups agreed to maintain a 'project log'. The log was a file into which we would put items such as the programme outline, an initial statement written by the tutor describing the background to the establishment of the particular RAP group, group members' biographical details and their Personal Development Plans, end-of-term evaluations, a record of tutorials and so on. These logs were to be the main focus for a collaborative reflection on the part of the co-tutors for that particular RAP group. Periodically, the partners would stop to reflect on the progress of the group by examining the evidence collected in the project log and then writing an agreed critical narrative which would point the way to changes they might want to make to their practice as group leaders or to the structure of the programme in that particular school. The logs would also be used as 'case records' (Stenhouse, 1978) that were subject to periodic meta-analysis, which was fed back into the discursive process of the team as a whole.

Additional data gathering. During the life of the research project there were three episodes of additional data gathering. The first took place towards the end of the first year and involved the gathering of comprehensive data

71

through a series of observations of RAP groups in action and follow-up interviews with 'key informants' (Burgess, 1985) in each of the five groups represented within the research project. These data-gathering activities were carried out by Judy Durrant on behalf of the tutors in the research team, although she also had a research agenda of her own. We opted for a semi-structured approach to the interviews, but Judy was also encouraged to adopt a conversational style in which she could draw upon both her personal experience of membership of a RAP group and her insider knowledge of the tutors' perspectives acquired through her membership of the ESACS team. Through her full participation in the research team meetings, Judy had developed a high level of 'theoretical sensitivity' (Strauss and Corbin, 1998) which we did not want to waste by the imposition of a rigid data gathering methodology. The outcomes of this first major data-gathering episode fed into our critical conversation as a team and contributed to the realization that the weak link in our scheme was our understanding of the role of the managers: those who were outside the RAP group but who would be approached by members of the group who needed to consult them about their priorities and plans. We decided to focus on this problem.

The second episode of additional data gathering involved focusing on an individual change agent in each of the project schools. The tutor concerned analysed the teacher's critical narrative about the process of change they had led, and then had a critical conversation with the teacher about it. A tape recording of this conversation was analysed to provide a basis for an interview with members of the senior management team focusing on that teacher's achievement as a change agent and the management arrangements that supported the change. A summary of the points made in those interviews was fed back to the teacher in the context of a further critical conversation. In this way we developed some in-depth insights into the way the school as an organization managed the process of change (see Chapter 7). The third episode of additional data gathering involved the evaluation of workshop and guidance materials through a telephone survey and a series of observations of group sessions where particular workshop materials were being used.

Data Analysis and Action

The ESACS project was an action research project. Our inquiry and reflection fed into action and changes in practice in at least three ways. First, we initiated single school cycles of inquiry, reflection and action; second, we initiated scheme-wide cycles of inquiry, reflection and action; and third, we engaged in wider discourse through publication of guidance and case study material.

Single school action research cycles. The co-leaders of each of the RAP groups represented within the ESACS project kept their own project logs and used them as a basis for regular evaluation of the programme. It was recognized that each pair of tutors would develop their programme according to changing circumstances and in response to developments within the school. The project logs would also be fed by the interview and observation data collected across the five schools represented in the ESACS project.

Scheme-wide action research cycles. The core research team's conversational process was itself an engine for change in that the data from the five schools and insights derived from the single school action research cycles were discussed in our regular evening meetings. This led directly to fresh innovation such as the decision to launch CANTARNET (Canterbury Action Research Network), a conference held each term for participants across the scheme, and the network journal, *The Enquirer.* Our discussion about professional discourse, fed as it was by the observations of group sessions and our own reflection about the discourse within the tutor team, led to the question of how we could extend the discourse for participants both internally and exter-nally. Internally, the discourse could be enriched by supporting the development of more effective structures for communicating the outcomes of individuals' development work; externally, it could be enriched by establishing networking arrangements. This sort of development was within our control, but there were other developments that required the response of those outside the research team.

The issue about the role of managers and their capacity to respond adequately to the participants' need to consult and negotiate about their priorities and plans emerged very strongly from the data. Our frequent and detailed discussions about the problem were all recorded in the written accounts of meetings which were sent to all the sleeping partners and copied on to the headteachers concerned, but, perhaps not surprisingly, no action flowed from this. In order to try to achieve some purchase on this problem, we resolved to take our dilemmas to the senior managers in the five schools. We were tempted to write a report and send it to the headteachers, but we thought that it would be more productive to hold a seminar at which we could engage the senior managers in a critical dialogue aimed at the improve-ment of the organizational culture of their schools. We planned an event that we thought would be attractive to the senior managers. We chose a hotel with a suitable conference room and good catering facilities. The event would begin in the afternoon with tea and would continue into the late evening over dinner. David wrote to the headteachers inviting them and their senior colleagues to help us develop the scheme by entering into discussion about its operation. The letter included the following paragraph:

> I hope that our discussions will be far reaching and that there may some practical outcomes. ESACS is conceived as a collaborative action research project so we hope to be able to identify new strategies which can be implemented and evaluated in action. However, we should not allow any practical constraints on such strategies to prevent us from expanding our understanding of school improvement issues. If the seminar leads merely

to a better understanding of the issues and a greater awareness of the possibilities for practical action, then I think that we could regard it as successful.

(Letter to headteachers, March 1997)

In advance of the seminar, we sent out papers which included an account of our research to date and an overview of the latest version of the model. It was summarized in the form of 'key strategies' and 'fundamental principles' (see Chapter 3).

At the beginning of the seminar we tabled papers which summarized the data from our inquiry the previous summer. The data was presented in the form of bullet points under the following headings: 'Beneficial Outcomes for Participants', 'Beneficial Outcomes for the School', 'Key Problems' and 'Factors Supportive of Teacher-led School Improvement'.

We decided to use fiction, partly as a way of disguising people and schools and partly to make the presentation more interesting and powerful (Walker, 1981). The idea of fictional mini case studies was an approach we were familiar with through the production of facsimiles in the guidance material written to support the RAP process. We presented a number of such case studies, each of which was an amalgam of different experiences in the project schools. It was for each headteacher to judge the extent to which they made visible their recognition of the problems represented by the stories. In the tables of summarized points, our concerns about managing change were represented directly as in the following extract (Figure 5.3).

Figure 5.3

The Data Presented as Bullet Points

There is a problem with the effective management of the teacher as change agent because:

- there may be a lack of clarity about the responsibility for supporting, monitoring and liaising with the change agent;
- support may be interrupted when responsibility shifts due to reorganization;
- managers sometimes fail to show sufficient interest in the change agent's work;
- managers sometimes fail to play their part in the consultation and negotiation process;

- there may be a lack of clarity about responsibility for dissemination of ideas, proposals, issues arising from enquiry/development;
- managers sometimes fail to challenge and respond to the change agent's weaknesses;
- managers directly involved in supporting participants may have difficulty with role conflict.

(ESACS Project Case Record, 1999)

This approach can be seen to be potentially disruptive to our discussion, whereas the fictional approach exemplified in Figure 5.4 below is far more palatable.

Figure 5.4

Story B: Marianne

Marianne is a modern languages teacher who is just starting Module B of the Diploma in School Development. She has been teaching for three years and joined the school-based group because she wanted to continue to reflect on her practice as she did at college. She also thought that the qualifications would enhance her career prospects.

Marianne began the year enthusiastically with the idea of focusing her development work on the use of technology in modern languages. She knows that development of technology across the curriculum is part of the school's development plan. She was excited by the use of European satellite television programmes and a video-link with French pupils at her teaching practice school. She had some initial ideas for inquiry, for example conducting an audit on the use of technology across the department, talking to other departments to see if it would be possible to share resources, and visiting some other schools to gain further inspiration.

Her head of department was generally supportive of her joining the RAP group as he recognized that the scheme would support professional development within the school context and this was bound to have a positive effect on her teaching. However, when she approached him with her ideas he was reluctant to give her full support. He said that the department couldn't cope with any extra changes at the moment and that it was unrealistic to ask staff to do any more work, especially with OFSTED next term. He was also worried about the extra costs that might be incurred. He suggested that Marianne confine her inquiry to her own classroom and scale it down as he thought the scheme was about personal professional development and should not have to involve other people.

Marianne came to her next tutorial feeling very discouraged. She had been hoping to broaden her experience by choosing a focus beyond her own classroom. Now it seemed that she would have to shelve all her ideas and interests. She wondered if the tutor could have a word with her head of department on her behalf.

(ESACS Project Case Record, 1999)

The seminar was successful in the sense that it opened up the issues and began to involve the headteachers more directly as partners in our research endeavour. The conversation was not particularly conclusive, but all present agreed that such an event should become a regular feature of the relationship between the HEI and the project schools. We had begun to establish a more purposeful dialogue with the schools, and hoped that it would eventually lead to an adaptation of the RAP model which would delineate a much more positive role for the school as an organization.

Engagement in wider discourse through publication. Our primary aim had been to improve our own practice as tutors and to develop the particular scheme in Kent, but it became clear early on that we had a responsibility to share both practical strategies and our understandings about the model, the context of its use and the possible benefits of it. Consequently there has been a steady stream of publications including conference papers, journal articles and chapters in books. In 1997, David produced what seemed at the time to be a definitive guide to the RAP model and its operation (Frost, 1997). This has been used to support a variety of experiments with the model in a range of different contexts, only some of which we have any detailed information about.

This volume contains case study material which will enable those who may be considering using the model to learn more about it. Educational situations are inherently complex and this has to be recognized in the methodology used to examine them. Some would say that this is best done by focusing on particular instances (Stenhouse, 1985; Simons, 1996). Clearly the extent to which ideas and conclusions from one situation can be applied more generally is problematic, and it is important to emphasize that the operation of the RAP model has been different in each school. Schools are unique and each school-based group has been established under a particular set of circumstances and conditions. Furthermore, individual teachers and the pattern of their particular developmental goals are also unique. It is impossible, therefore, to claim that valid and reliable generalizations can be made about the impact of the process, either in schools or for individuals. We do not see the model as a blueprint, but rather we believe that its strength lies in the power of teachers to use it flexibly to address their own concerns. We hope that the model hands the initiative back to teachers and schools. Drawing together the evidence and considering the emerging issues thematically, we illustrate and explore them in more depth by returning to case studies of a school which has embraced the model (Chapter 6) and through accounts of individual teachers' development work (Chapters 7, 8 and 10).

Conclusion

As we said at the beginning of the chapter, we needed to develop and articulate for ourselves a common understanding of the scheme and its impact on teachers and their schools, and this required a continuous, critical conversation which turned out to be irrepressibly naturalistic in spite of the institution of a variety of planned strategies and structures.

Looking back over our activity as a research group over a period of five years or so, we can see that this conversational thread was both extremely productive but also very inefficient. In order to try to explain this for ourselves, we listened to some of the tape recordings of our meetings and explored the way in which the structures and values of conversation had helped to shape the process and our agenda. Firstly, it seems clear that the *politesse* of conversation ensures that, although it may be a very satisfying form of discourse, it is nevertheless a most inefficient one judged purely in terms of the extent of progress of the planned deliberation. The rules of conversation demand, for example, 'turn-taking' and 'adjacency pairs', to use the parlance of socio-linguistics (Cortazzi, 1993). The first of these terms is fairly self-explanatory, but it is worth noting that turn-taking is more than a matter of equity in terms of the frequency or length of contributions; there are also questions of how the content of the conversation and the roles of the actors determine the legitimacy of each turn. Adjacency pairs, according to Cortazzi, are pairs of utterances contributed by different speakers but which constitute a coherent sequence often consisting of 'narrative' and 'receipt' (1993: 27). This means that, if politeness and therefore solidarity, are to be preserved, each utterance has to be followed by a number of others. The politesse characteristic of all conversations is confirmed and compounded in this case by the shared values inherent in the action research tradition; for example, the concerns with personal empowerment, collaboration, emancipation, democracy and the importance of addressing issues which are relevant to the action researchers themselves. In our own case we deliberately sought to create a mutually supportive climate in which it was considered legitimate to privilege immediate concerns over planned agenda items. We had talked quite early on about our meetings as 'guilt-free zones', for example. We can best illustrate the nature of our deliberative process by portraying typical episodes through fictional vignettes which have been validated by those attending the meetings (Figure 5.5).

Figure 5.5

The Conversational Discourse

Vignette 1

During a meeting, Gary apologizes for bringing up an issue which he thinks could be construed as too minor or merely tangential to our concerns; he seems hesitant and even a little distressed. David feels obliged to reassure him by saying that, if the issue is of concern to Gary, it is important for the team as a whole. Others nod and murmur assent. Following this, Michael feels moved to support David's view which he does by telling an anecdote about a staff meeting when he was a head-teacher; the story neatly illustrates how a seemingly irrelevant topic can in fact take a group's thinking forward. Judy seems impatient and, once Michael's story has reached a conclusion she cuts in quite abruptly and says: 'So, what is the issue Gary?'. By this time Gary feels confident enough to explain the issue which requires him first to sketch in something of the background to the problem. Following this, three of the four other people present demonstrate in turn that they understand the issue by recalling comparable events. The episode probably lasts for about twenty minutes.

Vignette 2

Before the meeting has started Michael generates a convivial atmosphere by starting a conversation which is focused on concerns which are inter-esting to us all. He says something like: 'While we are waiting for Gary to arrive let me tell you what happened at our RAP group meeting last night, it really illustrates perfectly what you said last week David about the need to penetrate the organization of the school.' He goes on to recount events which include conversations with both the headteacher and the senior teacher with whom he collaborates to lead the RAP group. These conversations indicate that the two individuals have completely different perceptions of the way that new ideas are consid-ered by the school's decision making apparatus. The story is engaging and we all begin to ask questions about it. Gary arrives a few minutes late and looks confused so Judy tells him that Michael was just telling us about the events at such and such a school. Gary then asks questions to try to identify the issue for himself. Rosanne then introduces a compli-cation when she says that the head only says that kind of thing to Michael because he is an ex-headteacher himself and that she is at a disadvantage because she has no access to such information. Michael seems to sense that Rosanne is slightly offended by this discrepancy and so tries to mend the situation by assuring Rosanne that this is precisely why it is important that these RAP groups are led by two people working in partnership, and that he would always share any insights he might gain access to because of his particular vantage point. At this point, David begins to shuffle his papers and points out that the meeting is half an hour old and the first item on the agenda has not yet been addressed.

Clearly this sort of conversation takes an inordinate amount of time and tends to make it difficult to follow the agreed agenda. The conversation helped to develop our understanding of the sorts of issues we all faced in working within the school-based scheme and it helped to build a sense of collegiality and solidarity. On the other hand, it held up the discussion of the more formal steps in our action research process and undermined our attempts to focus on decisions that needed to be taken if our planned research strategies were to be carried out within a reasonable time scale. These discussions were enriching and satisfying, but were at the same time seen to be exasperating particularly by the person who had to take action and needed to clarify a strategy or make a decision. It is significant that one of our number, Michael, who had a great deal of experience of teacher support and action research-based curriculum development, consistently argued that we could focus on the conversation as the main strategy for sharing accounts of practice and for engaging in collaborative reflection on the issues. There have been others who have argued for the validity of such alternative approaches (Johnston, 1994; Chang-Wells and Wells, 1997). His was a minority view which tended to be overwhelmed by the view that we needed to be engaging in an activity which would be more readily recognized as research. Given that Michael had been a headteacher for well over twenty years, it is doubtful that he shared the academic aspirations of those of us who could be said to be at the beginning of our careers as researchers.

One of the most important lessons for us is that action research is not simply a technical process which can be represented diagrammatically as a series of steps, but it is a conversational process which enables those participating to explore their understanding within a discourse governed by the rules of what the social theorist Habermas (1981) has called, 'the ideal speech situation'. These 'rules' have been summarized in the following way.

1 Each subject who is capable of speech and action is allowed to participate in discourses.
2 (a) Each is allowed to call into question any proposal.
   (b) Each is allowed to introduce any proposal into the discourse.
   (c) Each is allowed to express his attitudes, wishes, and needs.

3   No speaker ought to be hindered by compulsion – whether arising from inside the discourse or outside of it – from making use of the rights secure under 1 and 2.

(White, 1988: 56)

These rules of discourse can be used as a yardstick against which to judge the quality of our deliberations as a research team but also the quality of the discussion within the RAP groups themselves. What has been apparent about the RAP group discussions is that they are characterized by low levels of 'micropolitics' (Hoyle, 1986) because the participants set aside the territorialism and hierarchy of their institutional roles and relationships to work within a particular ethical framework.

So, as a research team, we would want to claim that it was not simply the knowledge generated by data gathering that empowered us, but rather, it was the discourse that enabled us to develop both confidence and self-doubt. We were able to move forward because we were able to engage in a discursive process that was increasingly challenging as it became more familiar and safe. Paradoxically, the seemingly comfortable conversational approach helped us to develop a sharper critical edge.

How then can the action research tradition constitute a resource for professional and school development? We are suggesting two apparently contradictory things. First, action research needs to be reconstructed as an efficient process, recognized as businesslike by teachers and school managers and rooted in the real world of schools as organizations with all that implies about collaborative planning and strategic thinking. Second, it should not be reduced to a technical process of action, data gathering and analysis, but it should be seen rather as a matter of critical discourse nourished by inquiry which is as systematic as we can make it within the limitations of available resources. We believe that, within the reflective action planning approach, there is the potential for the reconciliation of this apparent contradiction. We suggest that it is not sufficient for individual teachers to become more critical about education and about their practice; neither is it sufficient for teachers to integrate into their practice more systematic and organization-focused approaches to action planning and data gathering. The main lesson we have learned about inquiry and change is that educational improvement depends not on the wholesale importation into schools of the logic of school effectiveness research but on the nurturing, within schools and other professional contexts, of critical discourse through such schemes as we describe in this book.

6 Working with the Model

One School's Story

A key feature of the reflective action planning (RAP) scheme as it operates in Kent is that each school-based programme is a bespoke arrangement. There are essential elements determined by the model but the precise arrangements to support the reflective action planning process are the results of negotiation between the HEI and the school. It is also the case that each programme develops and changes in an organic way as group membership changes and as other internal factors come into play. In this chapter therefore, we want to explore the way these groups work by presenting a case study of the model as it operates in one school – St James', a co-educational, comprehensive school in an urban area.

We did not choose this school because it is typical, although most of the issues about the running of such groups did in fact arise in this case. We chose St James' because it was one of the schools represented in the research project set up to evaluate the RAP scheme (the ESACS project; see Chapter 5) and so we had collected data systematically in this school. It was also an advantage that all of us had first hand experience of working with that school's RAP group and had therefore discussed the issues at some length as part of our research process.

Setting up the Programme

The school became involved with the RAP scheme when Gary Holden was first appointed staff development co-ordinator. He wanted to try to overcome some of the problems associated with 'traditional', off-site INSET courses provided by external agencies. Typically, the teacher would return from such a course with ideas, but insufficient time, resources or opportunity to put them into practice (see Chapter 2). Gary wanted to put in place a programme of in-service activities more closely geared to the needs of the school and its staff.

RAP groups had already been established in several other schools, and there was increasing evidence of the model working successfully to support schools and individual teachers in their attempts to bring about school improvement through strategic planning, sustained systematic inquiry and critical reflection. It seemed that both individual and institutional needs could be met through the scheme. Gary circulated a proposal, and fifteen out of the sixty teachers on the staff expressed interest in participating. The first step was to find a tutor who would support the participants in their self-initiated inquiry. At the school's suggestion, the HEI approached a former LEA adviser turned freelance consultant, who had worked closely with the school in the past and was respected by the staff. He agreed to take on the role, and a meeting was arranged in which Alan and Gary were to devise a programme of seminars for the year. Alan was to be tutor, while Gary would take on the role of in-school co-ordinator.

It was decided that the group would meet from 4.00 p.m. to 6.00 p.m. at least four times each term. One early difficulty was choosing an appropriate room. The sessions took place at the end of the teaching day so there was no shortage of classrooms, but Alan and Gary felt that an ordinary classroom might not be conducive to the kind of dialogue and discussion they envisaged. In the event a number of locations within the school were used at different times. The most successful venue was a small classroom used for sixth form teaching in which the tables were arranged in a 'boardroom' style, with an overhead projector available; the least successful room was a large, draughty 'open' area that was usually used for Year 11 assemblies with poor heating and uncomfortable seats and 'folding' examination style desks. Gary arranged refreshments, at first bringing in biscuits and cakes from home, but later asking the school canteen staff to prepare a plate of sandwiches and cakes and a large flask of coffee before each session. This was a common experience in other schools.

Planning the Programme

Planning the programme turned out to be problematic. The scheme requires that participants negotiate the focus of their development work with their line manager and other colleagues; rather than following a 'syllabus' for the group sessions, the programme is built around the interests and needs of the group members. The challenge for Alan and Gary, the group leaders, was to try to achieve a balance between the participants' need for new experiences which would stimulate them and develop their knowledge and understanding and the need for responsive discussion of a wide range of personal interests and projects. The former requires detailed planning by the group leaders in order to identify appropriate research literature and to devise workshop activities which provide structure for collaborative reflection. The latter requires flexibility and spontaneity as well as a breadth of knowledge and understanding on the part of the tutors. This is a tension which runs throughout the RAP scheme, but was perhaps exacerbated at St James' by what emerged as a significant difference of view between Alan and Gary in the early stages. Alan tended towards the view that participants needed to have key texts, largely from the educational management literature, identified as prescribed reading, with tightly organized workshops to reinforce the ideas in the literature. Gary tended towards the view that the participants needed more space to explore the particular issues arising from their individual development initiatives. During the first few months the programme could be said to have lacked coherence because of this difference of emphasis between the two group leaders.

Of course it might be supposed that the nature of the process could have been defined more clearly before the programme began; the two group leaders had the opportunity for planning meetings and the participants were consulted as part of that planning. However, our subsequent evaluation indicated that the participants did not necessarily know what their needs were at the outset and were not adequately equipped to make a judgement about the form the seminars should take. As the first term progressed, they became a little clearer as to the ways the group leaders could best help them. For example, one session featured an activity that Alan, the ex-advisor, had used previously on management training courses; it enabled participants to identify and understand their own management style. In the post-session evaluations, several participants said that this activity did not meet their needs at that time. The group leaders were naturally disappointed to receive negative feedback, but in hindsight it was a seminal moment. For the first time the participants were beginning to develop clear views about the nature and style of the group sessions. They wanted time to discuss their own professional concerns and to receive feedback from other participants on their views and ideas. They wanted support in making choices about strategic planning and data-gathering techniques. This was a particularly interesting aspect of the first year, and one which has continued throughout the life of the scheme at St James'. The participants are not so much concerned with taking 'off-the-peg' solutions and methods, but prefer to work through their own action plans using their fellow participants and the group leaders as critical friends.

How the Programme Worked

By the summer term of the first year, the pattern of the twilight sessions had become established. Participants would arrive one at a time, clearly tired after a long day's teaching. They would talk about the events of the day over coffee while waiting for the others. As the tensions of the day began to recede the conversations would become more animated, and these pre-seminar coffee and cake sessions were characterized by a great deal of good-humoured banter. The sessions rarely started on the stroke of four, but the group leaders believed that it was important to allow for this transition between the teaching day and the more reflective mode of the seminar to take place.

The first item on the agenda was normally the opportunity for participants to update one another, often in groups of three but sometimes as a whole group, on the progress of their development work since the last meeting. These accounts would take the form of short narratives, but, as the trust between group members grew, the questions and observations became more critical and challenging. In this way it was possible to observe how, over time, the participants came to rely less on the group leaders for the last word on their work and more on each other.

The middle phase of the seminar would usually take the form of a presentation followed by discussion. At the beginning of the year, these presentations tended to be devised and animated by one or both of the group leaders. However, as mentioned earlier, the group began to challenge the group leaders' judgement as to the validity and relevance of some of these activities. Gradually, these presentations came to be given by members of the group, with the group leaders taking on more of the role of chair. For example, one group member attended a conference in London on school effectiveness and school improvement, at which well-known figures such as Michael Fullan and Jean Rudduck had made inputs. He then spoke to the group about the ideas the conference had generated, shared papers and led a discussion about how these ideas could impact on the work of teachers at St James'.

A refreshing alternative to group leaders or participants leading discussions was the occasional visiting speaker. The group leaders believed this to be an important feature of the sessions as there is a risk in a school-based scheme of insufficient challenge and breadth of perspective. If the relationship in the group is overly supportive, then it is possible that participants merely confirm one another in their own biases and preconceptions rather than moving them forward or challenging their beliefs. Discussion can become limited by focusing on internal school politics rather than the wider issues.

The sessions tended to end with business items such as dates of meetings, tutorials or deadlines for written work. While discussions were often animated, occasionally heated but always polite, it was noticeable how tired the groups would become towards the end of the session. It is a lot to ask busy professionals to spend a full day teaching, then engage in an equally demanding but quite different form of mental activity for a further two hours.

Members of the tutor team have consistently sought to try to find ways of overcoming the problems associated with both the need for challenge and the over-reliance on twilight sessions. The most successful innovation has been the setting up of the Saturday CANTARNET conferences at the HEI each term, to which teachers from all the participating schools are invited. The conferences have enabled participants to network with colleagues from other RAP groups and to benefit from fresh input from national figures such as Louise Stoll and John Elliott who have spoken and led workshops. As well as varying the pattern of provision, the conference has the effect of reducing the ill effects of insularity (see Chapter 9).

Each participant is also entitled to tutorial support, amounting to three hours per year. Again, this takes place on the school site, either during a free lesson or after school. The tutorials give the participants the chance to talk through their work in detail, clarifying action, getting advice on inquiry methods and trying to solve practical problems. During the first year Alan and Gary shared the tutorial responsibility, with the meetings usually taking place in Gary's office. During the second and subsequent years, Gary took over full responsibility for tutorials. As he was also a senior manager in the school, this brought with it certain dilemmas. On one occasion for example, a participant was experiencing some resistance from her head of department to the work she wanted to do. One of the central precepts of the scheme is that the focus for development initiatives should be negotiated with line managers. However, in this case the teacher was not able to negotiate at all. Gary could have used his position in the school to intervene, but this would have contravened the 'code of ethics' that governs the scheme (see Chapter 3). This code is designed to maintain confidentiality and protect individuals from 'repercussions' from things they might say during group sessions or tutorials. Gary saw his role as that of advisor on strategies she could employ to open up a channel of communication.

The HEI supplied the school with a 'book box', containing around fifteen texts, embracing books on school improvement, curriculum development, action research and so on. In subsequent years more books were added, with the HEI and the school making contributions. The books were made available to all staff, but in practice they were only used by RAP group participants or Initial Teacher Education (ITE) students. In addition, a visit to the library was organized during the first term so the participants were able to claim library rights and were introduced to the facilities including the computerized catalogue, which was also accessible on the Internet from the school.

The Development Initiatives

At the end of the first year we conducted an audit of ongoing development work and an evaluation of the RAP programme. An examination of participants' portfolios at that time revealed a range of successful development initiatives, a selection of which are described in brief below.

Developing a Whole School Behaviour Management Policy

Susan, a middle manager, had been asked by the senior management team to lead a small team of teachers in the development of a whole school behaviour management policy. She and her team interviewed colleagues, parents and students about their views on rewards and sanctions. She read about behaviour modification and about managing change. The team presented their evidence and proposals to the whole staff during a development day; they redrafted their proposals in the light of these discussions.

Developing Schemes of Work for GCSE Electronics

Bill, the head of the craft design and technology department, developed schemes of work for the first year of a GCSE electronics course and evaluated them in action. For each assignment, he devised a task sheet which required the students to evaluate each stage of their work. He was able to use these evaluations to compile an interview schedule to explore further what and how the students were learning and how they responded to the material he provided. The interesting feature of this project was that the evaluations and the interviews were in themselves learning experiences for the students as they were required to think systematically about their work and make explicit to themselves what they had learnt.

Target Setting and Academic Tutoring

James, a biology teacher, began a process of development which continued to engage him over a three-year period. He was concerned to develop target-setting procedures as part of tutorial work with Year 12 students. Like Bill, he devised activities which both provided him with data, and at the same time engaged his students in valuable learning experiences. The issue arising here – the degree to which students are not so much 'subjects' of teachers' inquiry, but can become partners in their own and their teacher's learning – provided a stimulating focus for discussion in one of the RAP group sessions. James asked his A Level students to keep journals over a period of one term in which they were to record 'critical events' in their learning; these then formed the agenda for the regular one-to-one tutorials. He used their journal entries to help him reflect on and improve the strategies he had devised.

Developing the Teaching of Poetry

Linda, an English teacher, wanted to make her teaching of poetry more exciting, so she developed a series of workshops, activities and visits for one of her classes. She asked a colleague to accompany her and the class on a visit to the Poetry Library in London to observe and talk to the children about their experience of the visit and the poetry workshop. She assessed the impact of the project by looking at the students' poetry writing before and after the visit and analysing observation and interview data which reflected the students' changing understanding and perception of poetry.

Evaluating the Programme

Interviews carried out with participants as part of the ESACS research project threw up a number of interesting issues which included the following points. First, participants said that the process of reflective action planning helped them to put their professional values into practice; in some cases this involved changing their practice and in some cases it was more a matter of developing the confidence to disagree with aspects of the national curriculum guidance and to exercise an independent professional judgement. One respondent reported that, through systematic planning and reflection, he had gained a sense of professional ownership of his curriculum area which he feared he had been losing.

Participants highlighted the importance of the group sessions which were seen as a 'safe' forum. The perceived absence of a 'management' agenda meant that participants felt in control of the meetings and of their content. They experienced an atmosphere of trust and mutual support within which they could:

- discuss issues openly and gain a better understanding of the perspectives of colleagues from other areas of the school;
- meet colleagues from different departments and discuss whole school issues;
- learn about and debate wider educational issues.

Participants claimed that, because they were able to comment critically on each other's development projects within the RAP group, their work tended to become increasingly systematic and founded on a firmer theoretical base. Also, participants highlighted the idea that discussions based on data involved a greater access to and acknowledgement of students' voices.

However, the scheme did not suit all those who originally enrolled. Three of the original group withdrew during the first term. Nigel, a science teacher who gave up after one term, said that he had joined the scheme hoping it would support the curriculum development work he was already engaged in on behalf of his department. For him the process of planning, action and review did not 'work'. He wanted the scheme to provide him with more specifically focused 'tools' with which he could work to carry out his development work. This links closely to the content–process issue discussed earlier in this chapter. The programme had eventually become a framework of support for teachers' inquiry-based development work in which it was assumed that the specific content of the development work, in Nigel's case a revised scheme of work, was a matter for the teacher to work through in consultation with line managers and colleagues. The group leaders did not see their role as subject advisers but Nigel wanted the programme to help him enhance his knowledge of the national curriculum in science. Clearly, the group leaders cannot be experts on all areas of the curriculum and so are not able to meet the needs of those teachers who want a programme which will give them direct teaching and updating of skills in their own curriculum area.

The Second Year: Changing Tutors, Changing Methods

In the second year, Alan left the scheme and Gary took on the role of tutor alongside David Frost, who joined him as co-tutor. Again, a key issue in planning the second year of the programme was to find the most appropriate balance between process and content. David and Gary believed strongly that the participants themselves should continue to have greater input by leading parts of seminars on a more systematic basis and by taking it in turns to evaluate each session rather than simply filling in a general evaluation sheet at the end of each term. To facilitate this, the tutors produced a two-page evaluation sheet which asked for comments on the practical arrangements, the appropriateness of the content of the session, the quality of discussion and the degree to which individual needs had been met. During each seminar, one participant filled in the sheet on behalf of the rest of the group. The nominated participant then read out to the rest of the group what he or she had written at the end of the session to confirm that it was a shared view. As well as introducing a research dimension into the running of the sessions themselves, and providing a forum for the group to discuss their needs, David and Gary found these evaluations immensely useful in ensuring that the sessions continued to meet the group's needs.

The joint tutoring arrangement was an innovation at the time, since in the other RAP groups in the scheme, the in-school co-ordinator did not take on a tutoring role. Most of the other in-school co-ordinators were responsible for administration, communication and 'domestic' arrangements such as organizing the accommodation and refreshments. However, once again this new relationship was not without dilemmas. The original aim had been to plan each session in detail collaboratively. Neither Gary nor David had committed themselves to this level of collaboration before. Gary and Alan had tended to share out the responsibility, taking turns to plan and run seminars. David had worked with several teacher-tutors previously, but he had tended to lead the seminar programme. David and Gary planned the basic outline of the programme together but, as the year progressed, it became increasingly difficult for the two of them to find sufficient time to meet and plan. This was partly due to the fact that David worked full-time in HE while Gary was a full-time school teacher, and so time during the working day was rarely available. How far could the relationship they had entered into ever be truly collaborative? The ESACS group meetings were invaluable at this time as they provided a forum where issues to do with tutoring the project could be discussed at a relatively profound level (see Chapter 5). Both David and Gary believed that even though there was limited time and opportunity to discuss and plan the St James' sessions in as much detail as they would have liked, these meetings did enable them to explore their values and reach shared understandings about the nature of their roles.

Notwithstanding all this, the evaluations provided by participants were positive, and both David and Gary felt they had gained personally and professionally from their partnership. Gary certainly gained in confidence as group leader. One participant described the way the two tutors worked together as a comic 'double act'. It is important not to underestimate the role of humour and 'fun' in those meetings. David became adept at presenting very crisp, enticing glimpses into key texts that had the effect of getting the essential flavour of a book across very quickly. David's main contribution, however, was that, coming from HE, he conferred a sort of credibility on the participants; increasingly they saw themselves not as teachers doing an INSET project, but as powerful change agents and teacher-researchers for whom reflective prac- tice had become a way of life.

During this second year the question of the impact of the participants' work on whole school development became of paramount concern to the tutors. For example, Susan's work on behaviour management the previous year had been warmly received by staff, senior managers and governors. The head particularly praised the systematic and inclusive way she worked, taking care to gather views and information from all areas of the school community and involving key staff in data gathering and the development of the policy. The scheme was therefore seen to be contributing in a very real way to school development as well as supporting personal professional development. At about this time, the head was interviewed by a member of the ESACS group. He felt that the participants played a crucial role in school improve- ment at St James' in that the innovations they proposed either at department or whole school level were the result of collaboration and careful assembling and analysis of evidence. He saw this as a model of professional and institu- tional development very well adapted to implementing and sustaining change.

Sponsoring the Teacher's Voice?

The impact of these individual development initiatives was recognized as significant, but the challenge then was to extend that impact by creating further opportunities for the change agents to disseminate their findings and proposals. The RAP scheme required teachers to present reports to interested professional audiences within the school, but in practice this was difficult to achieve. Frequently, a participant would find that he or she would be given a five- or ten-minute slot in a department meeting to describe a whole year's work. Of course, the RAP model assumes that participants will engage in strategic planning which involves identifying or even creating the events necessary for engagement with the school as an organization, but Gary felt that the school management could do more to create such opportunities. He was at this time curriculum manager at the school, and was therefore wrestling with the problem of how to encourage more teachers to engage in formal discussion about medium and longterm curriculum planning. As a consequence of these deliberations, he set up a working group to advise him on the development of the curriculum for the 14–19 age range. This group was to meet twice a term and was made up partly of colleagues who were invited to take part because of their roles in the school, for example the head of sixth form and heads of the larger departments in the school. However, a general invitation was also issued to any other staff who wanted to take part. Gary's aim was to provide a forum in which any interested teacher could have a voice in curriculum planning.

Three participants in the RAP scheme joined this group, and quickly found that they were able to feed their experiences of carrying out inquiry-based development work into these meetings. For example, the head of sixth form wrote in one of her critical narratives that she used the curriculum group meetings as a 'sounding board for my inquiry', and that she was in turn, 'able to obtain feedback from my questions and suggestions from a good range of interested and influential members of staff' (Rylatt, 1997). One of the other participants (Parsons, 1997) found the group less congenial, though no less important for her development work. As head of the technology department, she reported that she was initially 'despondent' at the unsympathetic response from other members of the group to her proposals for the place of technology in the Key Stage 4 curriculum, but felt that nonetheless the group gave her a forum in which to present her analysis of pupils' and parents' perceptions of technology and her arguments.

The other members of the senior management team realized that the 14–19 Group was becoming an effective forum for discussion and decision making and they began to set up similar working groups of staff to advise them on their areas of responsibility. For example, Annette, another senior teacher, formed a group to help her carry out research into equal opportunities in the school prior to writing a report for the governors. Once again, this group contained members of the RAP group. It was clear now that, after two years, the scheme was beginning to have an impact on whole school planning, since participants in the scheme were putting themselves forward to take part in whole school decision making.

The Third Year: Developing Peer-Group Support

In the third year, Gary became sole tutor of the diploma group. The group now included ten participants who were at different stages of the master's programme. Gary was concerned that it would be difficult to tutor a group made up of three 'beginners', four at the second stage of their post-graduate diploma and three at the master's phase. In practice, what began to happen was that the participants themselves took much more responsibility for the content of seminars. In the first and second years, the expectation from the group had been that each seminar would contain some form of presentation about an educational issue of topical interest, or advice on research methods, given either by one of the tutors, a visiting speaker or a member of the group. Gradually, Gary became aware that the more experienced members of the group naturally took on a mentoring role in relation to the newer members, seeing themselves less as course participants and more as co-leaders. The nature of the group sessions was subtly changing. Increasingly, they were providing a forum where participants could support one another in presenting and challenging ideas, suggesting alternative approaches to a particular problem and relating theoretical perspectives to their own context. Participants felt less need for Gary to 'perform', valuing instead the opportunity to develop their own ideas.

According to participants' evaluations, the atmosphere of mutual trust and support was at this time unlike the relationships that existed in any other meeting in the school. The participants had chosen to join the group; their goals and targets had been set by themselves in consultation with line managers, not handed down from above, and there was a belief that whatever was said in the group would remain confidential. However, dilemmas remained. The most serious of these from Gary's point of view was, as mentioned previously, his own role. He had been a member of the senior management team since the beginning, but he had shared his tutoring role with someone from outside the school. Now, as sole tutor, how could he be sure that the best interests of the group were being served? Was there not a danger that he could, however unconsciously, manipulate the group so that instead of supporting them in their self-chosen development projects, he was in fact using them to further his own management agenda? There is no easy answer to this question, but participants are given every opportunity to raise concerns of this nature in confidential evaluation forms sent to the course director each term, and so far all members have expressed satisfaction with the level and nature of support given. The fact that numbers have remained constant throughout the life of the project is another indicator that the programme continues to meet individual needs.

In addition, it was important to try to ensure that the group sessions did not become either too comfortable or simply tired and routine. Gary tried to avoid these dangers by inviting other members of the network, both tutors and participants, to make presentations to the group during the twilight sessions.

The Question of Impact

Since September 1994 when the scheme was first set up in the school, twenty-five members of staff, including some non-teaching staff, have achieved awards ranging from certificate to masters level. At the time of writing, the group still has ten participants and constitutes a vibrant force within the school.

The 'visible' changes that participants have been instrumental in bringing about include:

- a revised and improved tutorial system for post-16 students;
- a revised and improved behaviour management policy;
- the introduction of a new modern foreign language at Key Stage 3;
- the introduction of a 'reading recovery' scheme involving parents;
- the setting up of a new Special Educational Needs department;
- the introduction of a 'peer counselling' scheme;
- the introduction of new schemes of work and assessment procedures in the curriculum areas of technology, English and science.

However, the impact of the programme goes far beyond the implementation of these kinds of initiatives. It has also had a tangible effect on the professional culture in the school and on the management arrangements. The headteacher at St James' has always maintained a keen interest in the RAP scheme in terms of both the individual projects and the ethos of the scheme as a whole. In the academic year 1998–9, he set up 'focus' groups for each of the major themes of that year's school development plan, each chaired by a different member of the senior management team. The role of the groups was to make suggestions as to how the aims of that aspect of the plan should be implemented, monitored and evaluated. The head was influenced by the reflective action planning process in setting up these groups; he asked members of the RAP group to join them so that the school development plan would benefit from a greater sense of ownership and involvement on behalf of the staff. It is hoped that this will increase the level of participation by staff in whole school developments, and lead to improved decision making based on careful collection and analysis of evidence.

We believe the impact of the scheme at St. James' School can be seen in four main areas:

(a) Many members of staff have achieved formal recognition through the accreditation system. The achievement of the Diploma or the MA in School Development is intrinsically satisfying and has helped to further their career development.
(b) There has been a transformation of the consciousness of individual participants; their professional development is evident in terms of knowledge of new practices, understanding of educational issues, and the acquisition of skills such as strategic planning.
(c) There has been a transformation of procedures and practices at departmental and school levels as a result of participants' willingness to play an enhanced role in school development.
(d) By adopting aspects of the RAP model in the school's development planning process, there have been increased opportunities for all staff to play an enhanced role in whole school decision making.

It has been assumed that all of the above lead to improvement in the quality of the educational provision in the school and to enhanced student learning outcomes, but it is only recently that we have begun to explore how this can be assessed and how the 'effect size' can be maximized. The management team at St James' did not seek in the early days of the project to link participants' development projects to student outcomes in any overt way. The criteria applied when evaluating the scheme had more to do with the degree to which teachers felt that it was meeting their own personal professional development needs and enhancing their sense of personal agency. However, Gary is now engaged in an exploration of ways in which the RAP participants conceptualize the relationship between what they do as change agents and the effect on students' learning. At St James' School and across the CANTIS scheme as a whole, there is now a greater concern to evaluate the work individuals carry out by developing a clearer view of the ways in which students' learning is enhanced by it. This is discussed in more detail in Chapter 10.

7 The Teacher as Change Agent
Andrew's Story

This book is about teachers as agents of change and this chapter aims to explore teachers' capacity to exercise leadership amd to initiate and manage school improvement work, through an illustrative case study. It is essentially a story about one teacher's apprenticeship as a change agent. Andrew's story was told in his own critical narrative account; it was then explored and developed in tape recorded critical conversations with his tutor and in research interviews with his senior managers.

Andrew entered the profession in 1992, a science teacher bringing with him the highest of recommendations from his PGCE course. In his second year of teaching he joined the school's Reflective Action Planning group, which supported him through his first experiences of initiating and managing development work.

A Focus for Development

At the beginning of his second year with the programme, Andrew experienced some difficulty in being clear about his personal development priorities. He felt that he was expected to continue with the small-scale curriculum development work he had been dealing with previously, but he was more interested in matters beyond his own classroom teaching and even beyond the science department. The RAP group provided Andrew with a forum within which he could explore his professional values and ideas about the school. He was concerned about what a number of colleagues thought to be high levels of pupil disaffection and low standards of pupil behaviour in the school; he believed that the selective system in Kent had led to low levels of expectation and a lack of respect for students. The school had a wide ability intake but, at the end of Year 8, the top 25 per cent of the ability range was selected for the grammar school; in Andrew's view, this had a demoralizing effect on the majority of the students, who were not selected and remained at the school.

Andrew had read about 'student councils' in the *TES* (*Times Educational Supplement*) and had begun to think about the impact that such an innovation might have on his school. His first step was to attend a one day course publicised in the *TES* article, and this enabled him to develop an historical perspective that linked the student council idea to the general development of human rights in the 1960s. This is how Andrew explained himself in a piece of critical narrative writing a few months later:

> The basic proposition [is] that it is easier to engender notions of respect, co-operation and tolerance in young people if the educational institutions they attend display such qualities in their treatment of the young.
>
> (Wright, 1996: 17)

Having rehearsed his ideas in the RAP group and with his tutor, Andrew finally put forward his personal development plan (see Figure 7.1).

Figure 7.1

Andrew's Personal Development Plan

Roles and Responsibilities

I have been contributing to the review and re-writing of schemes of work and see myself continuing to do so throughout the coming academic year. However, I am also a group tutor in Year 10 and I am interested in developing the pastoral side of my work.

Focus for Development

I recently read a report in the *TES* about Student Councils – elected student bodies – which give students a direct involvement in decision making in the school. I followed this up by attending a conference about citizenship and am now very keen to pursue this idea. It seems to present real opportunities for children to learn citizenship and to enable us to develop a greater sense of the school as an inclusive community. I would like to explore the possible development of a Student Council in the school.

I realize that such a development would demand management skills which I may not have and so would want to talk with RS (deputy head) about strategies for managing the consultation process and the implementation of such a project.

Development Priorities

I realize that the student council project, if it is approved, will be very time consuming especially in the developmental stage. The process of consultation would probably take the whole of the Autumn Term and would have to include presentations to the SMT (Senior Management Team), the whole staff and the Governing Body.

Once the consultation process is complete, I will be able to devote more time to reviewing science modules and would imagine being able to start the review of the Yr 7 series by March next year.

Within the protected environment of the RAP group, Andrew had been able to 'sound off' and explore his frustrations about what he saw as the blink-ered views of some of his colleagues. He blamed some of them for assuming that the non-selected pupils behaved badly because of their fundamental nature rather than because of the demoralizing effect of their circumstances. However, in his Personal Development Plan (PDP) Andrew chose his words more carefully, because this document was the first of many that would be shared with various groups of colleagues for strategic purposes. He had to consider carefully the nature of his audience and what he wanted to commu-nicate to them. But how would he begin this process of consultation?

Strategic Consultation

Strategic consultation is an essential element in the RAP process and one which is discussed explicitly within the group sessions as well as in individual tutorials. Like most of the schools participating in the RAP scheme, Northfields School had adopted the notion of 'line managers' linked to their appraisal system (Fidler, 1989) so the most obvious strategy for Andrew was to consult his line manager – the head of department – which he did as a matter of courtesy. However, as Fidler points out, the line management system does not translate easily into the school context because each teacher belongs to a number of teams; this worked in Andrew's favour in this case, in that it opened up a space for a more strategic approach to consultation. In tutorial discussions it became clear that, since the Head of Science's attention tended to be focused on his subject, it would be more productive for Andrew to seek out a colleague with more of a whole school perspective and one who had direct connections with senior management.

This judgement could be seen as part of a general view of the school climate which Andrew perceived to be on the cusp of significant change for which he was impatient. In Andrew's narrative, he had observed that there were two 'catalysts for change', one being the appointment of a new head-teacher some months before and the other being the school's first OFSTED inspection which had precipitated a review of many aspects of practice throughout the school. Andrew believed that there were a significant number of teachers who, in spite of occupying pivotal positions in the school, were entirely focused on 'maintenance' (Hargreaves and Hopkins, 1991) and had no apparent interest in school improvement. This matches with our experience that professional discourse in schools tends to be dominated by discussions which focus on problem solving of the immediate sort, concerned with particular incidents and procedural clarification. Here, as elsewhere, the evaluation of practice and engagement in critical analysis did not appear to feature strongly.

Andrew chose to take his personal development plan to one of the deputy heads, who was immediately struck by the potential of such a project and arranged a meeting with the headteacher. Clearly, a focus on the early stages of a development project such as this raises important questions about the agenda for change and the distribution of leadership within schools.

The Agenda for Change

The language we employ to talk about educational change (implementation, reform and so on) seems to suggest the dominance of the external reform agenda but the relationships between national reform and the personal agendas of individual teachers are complex and problematic. There is no doubt that the idea to establish a student council was Andrew's idea, and that it sprang from his perception of the gap between his educational values and general practice in the school. However, it is also true that the idea fitted well with the school development plan. This is not to say that the document headed 'Northfields School Development Plan' explicitly included the idea of a student council as such, but the idea was seen by the head to have the potential to take forward aims that were explicitly stated. She believed that aims such as 'raising achievement' could be pursued by cultivating a more participatory ethos. This connection between pupil involvement and achievement is fairly well established in the school effectiveness and improvement literature (Hopkins et al., 1996). So, in the headteacher's words, Andrew's proposal was 'going with the flow'; in her view, Andrew was making a contribution to a developmental thrust that was already on the school's agenda.

The student council initiative was 'going with the flow' in a broader sense too: the head was trying to effect 'a culture change' amongst the staff and imagined that such an innovation would have great potential to involve members of staff in a process of collaborative reflection. She said that a number of the pastoral year heads were already developing structures for student representation, and so welcomed the proposal as building on what they were already trying to do. More specifically, she believed that a student council would provide a mechanism for introducing a range of changes for which she saw the need. A good example of this was a move to 'open-access' for pupils before school and during the lunch break, which is discussed later in the chapter. Although Andrew said in the interviews that his project was 'used as a vehicle' for such changes, he also said that he did not feel used or manipulated. Neither did he see himself as being absolutely in tune with the new head, but he did see the situation as a fair alliance of interests. So to say that Andrew's personal development priority made a good fit with the school's development plan is to take a rather broad view of the idea of development planning, and it could be argued that the development plan exists not in the document but in the discourse which is manifest in the many conversations, joint reflections, transactions and deliberations between colleagues; also in the bargains struck, the understandings gained and the practices mastered as they argue about how to improve the school.

In the interviews, it was put to the head and deputy that it was unusual for such a junior member of staff to be allowed and encouraged to lead such a substantial innovation: Andrew had been teaching for less than two years when he made his initial proposal. But Andrew, the head and the deputy head firmly rejected any notions that change agents should necessarily be senior members of staff or established managers. For them, it was a matter of the particular qualities of the individual and, in their view, Andrew had the kind of self-confidence and chutzpah which amounts to leadership potential. Our investigations more generally across the scheme have shown that whole school projects such as Andrew's need the commitment and time that younger members of staff may be able to give to them, whereas established managers tend to be swamped by externally driven requirements and day-to-day maintenance. They have to maintain an overview, and therefore find it difficult to become heavily involved in particular initiatives. It has been argued that the landscape of innovation is changing (Hargreaves and Hopkins, 1994) and that innovations are more likely to be initiated by the headteacher as part of some statutory requirement rather than the result of attempts on the part of young teachers such as Andrew to realize their values in practice. This case study shows how the external agenda for change, the head's agenda and that of the individual teacher can merge and interact to shape the nature of change and development in the school. It also shows, however, that the initiative as well as the drive for change and improvement can rest on the shoulders of teachers as individuals.

Seeking Institutional Support for the Innovation

At the conclusion of Andrew's discussion with the head, she asked him to produce a discussion paper for the next meeting of the 'management group', a body which comprised the senior management team (SMT) and the pastoral year heads. Andrew's proposal was well received; it resonated with other initiatives on which some year heads were working, and the group as a whole was in step with the headteacher's thinking on the development of the school ethos. A questionnaire, which Andrew subsequently circulated to members of this group and a few others, clarified the basis of their support. It told him, for example, that management colleagues believed that the student council would play a major role in the shaping of the school ethos by valuing students, giving them a voice and securing their support for policy development. It would also provide a structure within which problems could be dealt with and extra-curricular activities could be organized, all of which would result in improved behaviour management and more effective marketing of the school to prospective students. He was also given the clear advice that 'it will only succeed if the majority of staff support it', and that the benefits outlined above could be used to persuade colleagues of the value of the idea (Wright, 1996).

Following this high level endorsement and guidance on ways to proceed, Andrew drew up an action plan which specified making a presentation to the rest of his colleagues at the next whole staff meeting and subsequently making a similar presentation to the governing body. So far it was clear that Andrew had the capacity for *personal vision building* which Michael Fullan stresses is the first of four 'core capacities' which form the foundation of effective change agentry (Fullan, 1993: 13). (Fullan's ideas about teachers as change agents were common ground amongst members of the RAP group.) The staff meeting presentation was critical in that it was the first step towards the second of Fullan's core capacities – *collaboration* – on which the innovation would depend. Andrew threw his not inconsiderable energy into the event; he produced a short, humorous video in which he tried to pre-empt the issues that colleagues might raise; he prepared a great many overhead transparencies and left his audience with a paper summarizing the main points. It was clear to his colleagues that he had made full use of his capacity for *inquiry* – the third core capacity – he had made a thorough study of his subject and was aware of a wide range of pertinent issues.

A Clash of Values

In spite of the fact that he had predicted the issues that would arise, and, in his view, had addressed them in his talk, Andrew was nevertheless surprised and shocked by the conflict that followed. Here was a painful lesson about the fallibility of empirical–rational change strategies (Bennis et al., 1969). It cannot be assumed that change will automatically follow the presentation of 'good ideas' since it depends on people's perceptions of, and responses to, these ideas, which are themselves built upon different value positions and vested interests and are not necessarily rational.

It was clear that the concept of 'democracy' was controversial; it was suggested to Andrew by one colleague that the very mention of the word would grant a licence to overturn teachers' authority, without which educa-tion could not proceed. What was particularly salutary for Andrew was that these comments could not be dismissed as mere heckling; they had been set out in writing following his presentation. This is how Andrew described the situation in his critical narrative:

In a tightly argued and cogent rationale my correspondent lauded some aspects of what I was trying to do, but attacked robustly much of it. It was inspiring to read in the sense that at least one member of staff did find the idea of student democracy as threatening as I had perceived they might.

(Wright, 1996: 20)

There was no escaping the fact that there was a fundamental clash of values highlighted by Andrew's proposal. Arguably, educational goals are under-pinned by values (Hopkins, 1996) and a review of the school effectiveness literature suggests a positive correlation between 'shared vision and goals' and effectiveness. In the London Institute of Education's review for OFSTED it stated clearly:

Research has shown that schools are more effective when staff build consensus on the aims and values of the school, and here they put this into practice through consistent and collaborative ways of working and decision making.

(Sammons et al., 1995)

There are alternative views, however, which suggest that a lack of such coherence can be productive (Argyris and Schon, 1996) and that organiza-tions actually need subversives (Ganderton, 1991). For Andrew, there was of course a dilemma in that he needed the support of the majority of his colleagues and hoped that his presentation had been effective in building such a consensus. He had then to cope with the real sense of hurt and frustration when conflicting educational values were expressed. Andrew and David discussed this in a critical conversation which was taped as part of our research (see Chapter 5):

Andrew: ... but I have also achieved so much personally in the sense of change and understanding a lot more about change management – things like 'you can't mandate what matters' – you can't mandate what is going to be important. You've got all these ideas of what's important and you want to say 'this is important' but other people have got their ideas about what's important and you've got to be willing to change your agenda and be flexible ... and ... it's diffi-cult this but ... you've got to be flexible but also driven continually by the same values.

David: So you are saying that improvement comes from a process of clari-fying values and a commitment to change.

Andrew: Absolutely.

In the end Andrew was able to reflect positively on the experience because he held strong democratic values and, as Barry MacDonald reminded the research community recently, 'Democracy is not about consensus, it's about argument' (MacDonald, 1998). Democracy also entails the toleration of difference. In interview, Andrew recalled in particular an in-service session held in January 1996 to prepare for the launch of the student council; he had observed and marvelled at the way his colleagues, some of whom he had perceived to be uninterested in school improvement, engaged in spirited critical reflection and argument and concluded that this development work was contributing to the development of a more *collaborative culture* in the school (Fullan and Hargreaves, 1992).

Vision and Planning Come Later?

With the benefit of these harsh lessons, Andrew rewrote his initially optimistic action plan and talked it through with the deputy head. The time-scale of the development period was lengthened to allow for thorough consultation with all interested parties. Following the presentation to staff, a Student Council Working Party consisting of students, teachers, governors and parents was established under Andrew's leadership. The working party met four times to discuss possible models and structures. These discussions were based on data which conveyed the views of all and illuminated models in operation in other schools. It was not until the end of the spring term that elections finally took place enabling the Northfields School Student Council to meet for the first time at the beginning of the summer term.

The headteacher did not agree that such elaborate consultation was necessary and, in retrospect, Andrew thought that she may have been right; the momentum had been severely challenged in the autumn term through the divergence of views and values expressed by colleagues, and it might have been better to have plunged into action sooner and then to have adjusted practice in the light of feedback. In the taped critical conversation, Andrew quoted one of Fullan's slogans: 'Vision and Strategic Planning Come Later' (Fullan, 1993: 28). The argument behind this was that colleagues have to have an opportunity to get involved in shaping the vision through practice. Andrew had wanted to consult everyone to try to ensure a high level of consensus on the model adopted, but this may have been a false hope. His preferred launch date was the following September, the head pushed for the January before that, and in the end they compromised on April. It is interesting to note that the first term of operation saw fairly major changes to the model in the light of the reactions in practice of those who had been consulted. The Working Party had decided that there would be 'Year Councils' that would discuss their own concerns and then delegate representatives to pursue those issues in the full 'School Council' but, when it came to it, not all of the year heads played their part.

Ongoing Evaluation

In the early stages of the development work, Andrew had tried to clarify his values and translate them into a form which would make possible some kind of ongoing judgement about the validity or success of the innovation. An example of these 'principles of procedure' (Peters, 1959; Stenhouse, 1975) was: 'to empower students across the school to see participation and action as routes to solve problems, as opposed to blithe acceptance and passivity' (Wright, 1996: 11). These statements were an attempt to articulate Andrew's aims which served as a starting point for investigation and discussion. The Working Party discussed the principles and used them as a basis for judgement about models and structures. Later, Andrew wrote for himself four 'possible indicators of School Council impact on the institution', for example: 'Students perceive that the School Council represents their legitimate voice and that changes occur as a result of its existence' (Wright, 1996: 33). This helped him to monitor progress within the first term of the Council's operation through interviews with Councillors and an analysis of the minutes of the Council meetings.

Leadership and Resistance

The deliberations of the new student council threw up some very challenging issues for the school. For example, student councillors frequently brought up issues concerned with the performance of individual teachers and these were mostly deflected, students being advised to take these matters up with the relevant year head. Andrew followed the matter up by discussing with the year heads possible mediation procedures for students with particular grievances. When the head subsequently invited the School Council to 're-write the school rules', students argued that 'if the kids have to have rules, why don't teachers?' In consultation with the head, Andrew took statements from the school's behaviour management policy and set them out in poster format as a 'Staff Pledge'. It said that staff would 'treat all students with respect and in return expect to receive respect', 'apply the student code of conduct fairly', 'use merits, rewards and praise consistently' and 'mark all work promptly and constructively'. This poster was distributed to all staff, who were asked to display it alongside the new code of conduct for students. However, a subsequent tour of classrooms revealed that, in the majority of cases, teachers had declined to display the pledge.

Councillors also became involved in the devising of an anti-bullying policy and discussions about the lunch queues. When the Staff Association protested at the head's new request that members of staff should refrain from jumping the queue, the School Council was cast as the demon of the piece. Andrew responded with an article in the school's weekly newsletter defending the Council. The student councillors interviewed by Andrew spoke positively about these developments. He wrote:

Throughout my discussions with school councillors I gained an over-riding sense of the debt of privilege they felt they owed to an institution which was willing to give them a voice. This was expressed to such a degree that councillors became involved in heated exchanges with students who disagree with some decisions of the management which the school council had supported.

(Wright, 1996: 41)

So, the students, or at least the councillors, were gradually becoming enfranchised, but some of the teaching staff seemed to believe that this was at their expense and some began to question the leadership of this young teacher who seemed to be responsible for so much change. Although the senior managers perceived Andrew to be successful in building relationships with his colleagues, Andrew himself reported the impact of considerable negative feelings towards him such that he felt that he needed to 'keep a low profile' for a few months. The headteacher recognized leadership qualities in Andrew (vision, communication skills, self-confidence, charisma), and the fact that the school now has a functioning School Council suggests that her faith in Andrew was not entirely misplaced, but clearly the ability to sustain leadership depends to a large extent on the authority derived from the formal position in the organization. According to Angus (1993), most of the literature on leadership assumes that leadership is exercised by people in appointed positions rather than individuals like Andrew who take on leadership roles in order to realize their values in practice. An examination of the minutiae of change enables us to conceptualize the school as an 'arena of struggle' (Ball, 1987) in which power is not simply exercised through formal leadership travelling in straight lines, but is a resource which is deployed by a range of individuals in complex relationship with each other.

Management of the Change Agenda

The example of the move to 'open access' for pupils illustrates how this worked in practice. The head told Andrew that she was concerned that many students were being effectively shut out of the school building in the lunch breaks and before school because of the accretion of various limitations on access, and that this had contributed to the development of negative feelings about the school; she harboured a plan to change this. She therefore asked him to 'drop' the issue into the council discussions. Andrew did this, and the students readily took up the issue as their own. At their next monthly meeting with the head, the councillors raised the matter and demanded a change in policy. The head naturally responded positively and an open access policy was duly implemented.

There is clearly collusion here between the head and Andrew in shaping the change agenda. A School Council discussion was prompted, which was then used to legitimate the head's policy initiative. The head's agenda was rooted in a school effectiveness perspective which has it that high pupil performance in examinations correlates highly with an inclusive ethos. This is essentially a consumerist viewpoint which is clearly linked to the government's social market philosophy (Elliott, 1996). Northfields School is in competition with other schools in the area including a grammar school and is judged by its position in the 'league tables'. Andrew's agenda was that it is undemocratic to lock the students out of the school, and that citizenship can only be learnt through inclusive practices. The students' agenda may well have been that it is more comfortable to be in from the cold. The change in policy does not necessarily arise from a coherence of values, but is the product of alliances and the coincidence of a range of mutually convenient goals and purposes. So it may well be that 'unity of purpose' and even 'shared vision and goals' (Sammons et al., 1995) can still be developed even if there is a diversity of educational values.

A Personal Professional Agenda?

As part of a micro-political perspective (Hoyle, 1986), one might want to suggest the possibility that for Andrew there is another, more personal agenda which is concerned with the gratification of his own needs and the pursuit of his career development. There is general agreement evident in the data that Andrew learned a great deal about management through this adventure. His head talked very positively about Andrew's professional learning: learning about colleagues' sense of initiative overload, learning how to mount in-service events, learning how to deal with conflict and the emotional reactions of colleagues, learning how to sustain change by publicising positive gains, and so on. The view that Andrew had served a successful apprenticeship as a manager was confirmed by his subsequent appointment as curriculum manager, a senior post which embraced head of science and head of Year 9. Such advancement might well be seen as a reward for his co-operation with the head's agenda, a view that would undermine everything that has been said about change agentry and moral purpose. This possible interpretation was explored with Andrew in interviews, and his responses seemed to suggest that he was not motivated by anything other than his own commitment to particular educational values and a natural desire to realize those values in practice.

Focusing on the connection between leadership and agency aids our understanding of the process of school improvement, and the part that reflective action planning can play in it. Angus has argued most persuasively that:

> Those who hold administrative positions need to realize that their best contribution to educational reform may be to use the authority of their position to facilitate the exercise of agency of those of their staff who, for one reason or another, have begun to examine critically, and engage in

dialogue about, educational issues and educational purposes so that they are rendered problematic and subjected to scrutiny.

(Angus, 1993: 86)

This argument rests on a theory about leadership which is not drawn from the structuralist tradition in which leadership styles are underpinned by values such as control, predictability and efficiency. Angus prefers instead to talk about 'transformative leadership', which recognizes the complexity of rela-tionships in schools and, following Giddens (1984), he argues for the possibility that teachers, and people in general, have always played a significant part in 'shaping the conditions, structures, organizations, rules and agreements that shape their lives'. This power becomes a more 'free-floating' commodity which can be appropriated by teachers as they exercise their human agency.

Reflective action planning has an important role to play in supporting the process whereby individuals exert their human agency and take on leadership roles in relation to particular development initiatives. The following extract from one of the taped critical conversations between Andrew and David is illuminative.

David: What is phenomenal about your account ... You had only been teaching for two years when you set out on this bold initiative and you mentioned the problem of no status. How do you see that? You actually exercised a great deal of influence and so on here ...

Andrew: The point is that I see my ideas – well, they are not my ideas anyway, they are other people's ideas that I have read – they are just damn good ideas ... never mind that I am only two years into teaching – they are damn good ideas and I have got a lot of energy and excitement and wanted to try them out. I was just lucky to land in a school where the management was so supportive and gave me this opportunity and gave me the trust to say ...

David: You are saying that, one, you learned a great deal about managing change and two, you had the temerity to initiate change even though you had low status and a low level of experience but ...

Andrew: Precisely but that temerity comes from my basic belief in democ-racy, my basic belief that it doesn't matter how many years experience you've got, if you've got a damn good idea you should be given the opportunity ...

Andrew: This two years into teaching ... I don't see it as an issue. Other people see it as an issue so it probably is but ...

David: It's an issue about change though, isn't it, because, if you look at what's happening in schools and where the drive for change comes from, you find to a great extent senior management teams trying to initiate change with lots of people underneath saying 'I'm too busy', 'I don't agree with it' or 'They are doing it to us again' and so on – the reason your work is so interesting is that it demonstrates the capacity of ordinary foot soldiers as it were – somebody who has no status and power in the institution – to participate in the process of change management.

Andrew: Well stuff hierarchical structures as far as I'm concerned. Either we are all foot soldiers or we are all managers as far as I can see. I mean, I am not a communist – there's got to be disciplined procedures and structures but we all have the capacity and it's the job of a manager to develop the people around them because you need people that are wanting to develop all the time in many different ways and you need to encourage them.

David: I agree and I think that you have demonstrated very well that education is a moral purpose and we all have the capacity for leadership and managing change.

Giddens's theory of structuration (1984) is helpful in illuminating Andrew's work as a change agent. Andrew was able to deploy power to challenge the structures which constrained his practice and the way others deployed their power to resist and reshape the innovation. It was not straightforwardly a matter of his role bestowing on him the necessary authority to act, nor was the head able to wield power in a straightforward way. These two leaders were both part of an organizational mêlée in which change agents have to think and act strategically, making strategic alliances and taking opportunities to achieve steps forward. In Angus's words: 'it is through the dialectic of human agency and social structure that relations of co-operation, consent, or coercion are actively constructed' (Angus, 1993: 87). So Andrew has been able not only to implement successfully an educational practice, but he has also been able to contribute significantly to the professional culture in his school.

The Role of the Reflective Action Planning Framework

Of course, it could be said that individuals such as Andrew would have exerted their human agency regardless of the provision of support in the form of the RAP scheme. The headteacher said that she thought that Andrew would have done this sort of thing anyway. However, when the same question was put to Andrew, he said: 'Those people that will do it anyway, do it anyway, but whether it will be successful or not is the key question ... and maybe reflective action planning is the tool-kit they need.'

Investigations across the scheme suggest that individuals who were not at all like Andrew were nevertheless able to clarify and articulate their educational values, translate them into strategic planning and exercise leadership through a development process based on systematic inquiry. They were able to draw support from their membership of their RAP group; the group sessions provided a forum for rehearsing key steps in the change process and for exploring the issues arising from the management of change.

The RAP scheme can be clearly seen here to be supporting the teacher as a change agent. For Andrew, it was sufficient that a student council had been established and appeared to be giving students a voice in school development. The headteacher perceived substantial improvements in the school ethos which were related to the student council initiative and fitted well with her agenda as a new head. The innovation had a significant impact on what have been called the 'internal conditions' for school improvement (Hopkins et al., 1994). In Andrew's final critical narrative, he observed that the initiative involved colleagues in debate about values and the ethos of the school, a benefit that he had not set out to achieve, but the head had clearly anticipated this and, through good stewardship and the skilful distribution of leadership she had been able to move the school forward in this way.

8   Developing Teacher Professionalism Through School–Based Inquiry

Penny's Story

This chapter explores the role of teacher inquiry in the process of school improvement and considers the extent to which teachers have a part to play in contributing to, as well as applying educational research. We go on to illustrate with a case study the way in which the reflective action planning process increases the individual teacher's capacity to contribute to school development.

OFSTED's chief inspector, Chris Woodhead, is scathing in his dismissal of 'the cult of the reflective practitioner', where teachers seek to extend their professional learning through links with HEIs and their involvement in research and academic discourse. He believes that while a small number of outstanding teachers will 'simply get on with things in their own inimitable way',

> progress will be made if we focus our efforts, first, on giving the young teacher the practical knowledge and understanding he/she needs to survive in the classroom, and, second, on raising the game of the average teacher who, in mid–career, very possibly through no fault of their own, is not achieving the results they can and must.
>
> (Woodhead, 1999: 3)

In the current political climate, then, a mechanistic, technicist view of educational processes is often assumed. There is an unrelenting emphasis upon standards, narrowly defined and therefore conveniently quantifiable, and a move towards assessing and rewarding teacher performance based on indicators of student achievement. Within a competitive climate, as opposed to a collaborative culture characterized by shared understanding and mutual development, there is a tendency for the profession to be judged and undermined more than supported (Hargreaves, 1994).

The Researcher–Practitioner Divide

Educational research is under scrutiny. Those professing to engage in research activities are challenged with questions about the quality and validity of their work, its subject and context, its application and dissemination. There are questions over who conducts the research, who funds it, who has the power over what is researched and how the results are subsequently used. Despite the vigour of the debate in academic circles, it has been suggested that the impact of current research upon the consciousness and practice of individual teachers is minimal (Bangs, 1998; Barnard, 1999). Hargreaves recognizes dissemination of research outcomes as 'the unsolved problem':

> past attempts to improve communications, for example by the style and presentation of research reports, have made very little impact on users. Such approaches … fail to acknowledge, and do too little to close, the huge gap between the research community and practitioner communities.
>
> (Hargreaves, 1998: 9)

Teachers feel distanced from the wider educational discourse, and in some cases excluded from it (Learmonth, 1999). While policy may be billed as research-based, the research tends to be buried in the rhetoric so that it cannot be judged for what it is and 'denies the legitimacy of dissenting voices' (Elliott, 1996a: 200). Other research outcomes emerge through the media with the inevitable political 'spin'. The nature and context of the research data are usually inaccessible; its validity has to be taken on trust, yet questions have been raised about its quality (Goldstein, 1998; Hargreaves, 1996).

The profession is caught, powerless, between conflicting research paradigms (Reynolds et al., 1996; Stoll, 1996). Teachers are confronted with 'information' purporting to be based on research, in which the distillation is so complete that many of these points can be dismissed as mere platitudes. Elliott (1998) suggests as much in relation to the claims made by the school effectiveness movement. These include identification by Reynolds (1994) of 'enduring truths' in the processes that have been found to be effective through research, such as high teacher expectations, high levels of pupil involvement in lessons and other aspects of school life, and behaviour management through rewards rather than punishment.

Nevertheless, the thrust of current policy is to encourage stronger links between educational research and school development. Ideas about how this might be achieved involve a commitment to the introduction of structural change at national level. The Institute for Employment Studies report commissioned by the DfEE in 1998 emphasized the need for the creation of 'a more effective research system'. At the time of writing, the DfEE intends to commission two dedicated research centres, to support both large-scale quantitative studies and more qualitative investigations and to establish a system for the review and dissemination of research through a central database, as reported to the 1999 BERA (British Educational Research Association) conference (Budge, 1999). Hargreaves discusses ways in which HEIs and LEAs might co-operate in co-ordinating regional and national 'networks and webs for educational research and professional knowledge creation' (1998: 15) involving groups of schools at different scales. The TTA, whose remit includes raising the quality of educational research and increasing the demand for it amongst teachers, has established a panel of teachers to support research which is 'relevant to classroom practice' and to suggest ways of disseminating the results so that they are accessible to teachers (Barnard, 1999).

If teachers are to inform their practice with a much wider and deeper body of educational knowledge, they have to be convinced of the *value* of this. They need to know how to gain access to it in a manageable and relevant way and how to use it to increase their professional understanding in order to support their work. It is important for them to be able to make a genuinely critical response to published outcomes if they are to be empowered to act appropriately upon the evidence and information available. Furthermore, teachers need to be able to make meaning of such knowledge for themselves, in their own unique situations. This requires them to be equal and active participants in the discourse; they need to have a means of contributing directly to the generation and discussion of educational knowledge and understanding, rather than acting as mere recipients of knowledge produced by outsiders through what is often perceived as a remote academic process.

Rudduck (1991) takes us to the heart of the problem. Following the 1988 Education Reform Act, she found schools suffering from initiative fatigue and mounting bureaucracy, which have continued to exert relentless pressure ever since. She describes teachers beset by 'multiple initiatives whose coherence and whose relationship to their own values they haven't the time, and some-times the energy, to work out' (1991: 92). She believes that:

> Real curriculum development ... will not be achieved by teachers who feel so used and acted upon. They have got to feel some control over the situation and, in order to feel a sense of control, they have to recognize what it is in schools, classrooms and themselves that they want to change.
>
> (Rudduck, 1991: 92)

Change involves an acknowledgement of the need for the development of complex understandings through analysis and reflection, the working out of personal and communal professional values, the search for professional iden-tity. It can be informed by the outcomes of research but it cannot be imposed, and is unlikely even to be encouraged, merely by making certain 'findings' accessible.

Empowerment through Inquiry

We believe that the empowerment which comes from participation in and leadership of inquiry-based development enables individual teachers to become agents of effective and appropriate change for schools, extending and enhancing their professionalism. We have found that an inquiry approach to development can become part of the value system for individuals and groups of teachers which extends beyond the term of an accredited programme, and that this can be built into the school improvement process. While policy may be adjusted in support of a climate of professional knowledge creation, this can only have an impact upon teaching and learning when teachers have the capacity to act in ways which are meaningful in their own contexts. This involves exploration and inquiry at a personal professional level, but it is important that this is set within a climate of openness, collegiality and fluidity of structure in which the school's policy and practice can be challenged and changed. Internal and external networks are used to disseminate ideas and knowledge, to validate outcomes and to increase critical application through mutual 'tinkering', with the HEI providing a critical filter through which to assess content and process. Thus 'centre–periphery' research and development schemes and linear models of knowledge production, dissemination and application are supplanted by interactive processes which merge principles and practice and diminish the divide between researchers and practitioners.

The reflective action planning model provides a framework for systematic inquiry, in which investigation and application are inseparable and criticality and rigour are built into the process. Teachers gain control of the inquiry focus, tailor the investigation process to their professional situation and use this as a basis for strategic action to effect change in school, within the context of their professional responsibilities in relation to school development priorities (see Chapter 4). Transparency through negotiation, consultation and reporting is required so that the inquiry is subjected to the public scrutiny of those who understand the context best: those who are directly involved and are therefore able to authenticate and validate the evidence and its analysis (Somekh, 1995). Insularity is further counteracted by participation in school-based group discussion and additional interactions between colleagues beyond the scheduled meetings. The approach can become fully integrated with normal professional practice to the extent that teachers develop the continuing capacity for driving change and development based on the analysis of evidence from their own situations. Criticality is enhanced through collaboration within the wider educational discourse which draws together internal and external research, understanding and experience.

Integrating Systematic Inquiry with Professional Practice: A Case Study

We use a case study of one teacher's experience of five years of working with the reflective action planning model, to illustrate and explore some key aspects of the inquiry process used as a framework for individual 'change agentry'.

1   The relationship between individual and school development priorities.
2   Inquiry as integral to professional practice.
3   The centrality of reporting, consultation and collaboration.
4   Increasing the individual's capacity for change agentry.

Penny Skoyles was a participant in the School Development Scheme, and was awarded her Masters Degree in 1998. Her approach as a change agent and teacher–researcher is revealed through her writing for accreditation purposes and for wider publication (Skoyles, 1998a, 1998b; 1999; Sparke et al., 1998) and we have also drawn upon data from interviews conducted as part of the ESACS Project research (see Chapter 5), both with Penny and with her head-teacher. It is worth noting that in this case study we concentrate on the *process* of inquiry-based development rather than on the outcomes of the work; the question of impact is discussed fully in Chapter 10.

Individual and Institutional Development Priorities

When Penny joined the RAP group in her school, she had recently joined the staff, initially teaching part-time. She was used to adapting to the changing nature of her subject area of home economics/food technology, and had taught in adult education as well as in different schools. She wanted to make her lessons more practical and relevant, and therefore decided to focus on the development of new schemes of work with a particular year group, using the action planning approach to experiment with pedagogy as well as developing new materials. The programmes of study developed during this first year are still being used by Penny's department several years later.

Penny experienced a considerable increase in professional confidence during her first year of involvement in the programme. As well as becoming bolder and more skilled in trying out new ideas in her classroom, she was becoming less isolated amongst her colleagues. Although she would undoubtedly have become more established as a member of staff over time, as a matter of course, she has no hesitation in identifying her involvement in the programme as a major factor in enhancing her professional development, leading directly to her capacity to embark upon a more ambitious and wider ranging development theme in association with her next accredited module.

Penny's commitment to providing more meaningful and relevant experiences for her students and her courage in trying new ideas and approaches had previously been tested by a particularly disaffected group of students on a 'Caring' course which she tutored as part of the Youth Training Scheme (YTS). They did not respond to her initial attempts to engage their interest and attention. She was unconvinced by the YTS suggestion that students should be sent around the town in wheelchairs: 'they would just have gone home …'. Penny realized that these students needed authentic experiences, not 'scenarios', and organized a series of visits to homes for the elderly and disabled within the local community, where visitors were welcomed as a contact with the outside world. The students 'blossomed'; they began to take the initiative, talking to the residents and taking them for walks, and several continued to visit after the course had ended.

Another influence on Penny's thinking at this time was the way in which her initial development work prompted her to ask questions more widely, considering her professional development within the school context. She realized that colleagues were unaware of the work she had been involved in, that communication of ideas and best practice was limited and tended to rely on informal individual conversations. She recognized the importance of expressing her own interests and communicating ideas, encouraged by the reflective action planning model's emphasis on reporting to different audiences.

As her interest in links with businesses and the local community became known, she was asked by the newly appointed headteacher, on the recommendation of the senior management team, to become the link tutor for the cross-curricular theme of economic and industrial understanding. This became the focus for the next phase of her development work and opened up a channel of communication with the head which increasingly enabled Penny to introduce her own agenda for change, as she explained in an interview:

> It gave me an opportunity to talk to (the head) about not only my teaching but also my interests and what I would like to do within the school and be involved in within the school. And that was … to be involved in encouraging people to have links with industry, to find out what successful things other members of staff had done with industry, but also to get involved more with careers.
>
> (Interview data)

After being appointed as the link tutor with responsibility for co-ordinating 'industry links' and personal and social education (PSE) topics, Penny had an initial discussion with the senior teacher who was her line manager in this respect, and was then left to her own devices, reporting back periodically. Thus the focus for the development work was a successful marrying of individual and school priorities. Penny's inquiry provided evidence which led her to produce a formal report identifying ways in which careers education could be improved, suggesting more personal interviews with students and the introduction of more speakers from outside, and suggesting that PSE was losing value and was probably covered in the discrete subject areas. The report was well received with respect for the systematic way in which Penny had gathered evidence and presented it in written form. The headteacher spoke highly of Penny's contribution, saying in interview that she followed her own vision and made contacts, driving the work forwards; she had assumed authority and expertise in the area of economic and industrial understanding, and was seen as a person with ideas and an initiator of change.

This recognition led to Penny being asked to take on further responsibility. She was asked to assume responsibility for this area of the curriculum by conducting a further audit on cross-curricular coverage, collating a database and communications through the staff bulletin to record the use of outside expertise in order to make contacts more widely known and to enable staff to co-ordinate visits, and becoming involved in sixth form careers work. Penny welcomed this opportunity to exercise her interest and increase her influence; in addition, her status in the school increased and she was promoted internally.

With the third stage of her development work, Penny entered a further phase of professional learning. While she could have extended her inquiry on economic and industrial understanding, she decided eventually to focus on what had become a more pressing and challenging development task, the introduction of a new General National Vocational Qualification (GNVQ) course into what was traditionally an academic sixth form. This allowed her to play a major role in an important school development issue as well as strengthen her own position as a middle manager in charge of a 'vulnerable' curriculum area. Penny's account of this two-year development reveals how her previous experience and professional development through reflective action planning had changed her outlook considerably and raised the level of her thinking. She quickly realized that the introduction of the new course would uncover many wider issues, as some staff expressed resistance to a change in the type of provision post-16. The clash between Penny's values and the existing 'academic' culture of the sixth form became apparent and raised some fundamental questions for her: 'I was led to question the value of vocational education and felt the need to investigate further its very slow acceptance by the old system' (Skoyles, 1998a: 5).

She knew that the development work would involve much more than 'tinkering' within the walls of her classroom, producing new course materials and learning the appropriate skills to teach GNVQ. She set out deliberately to employ the reflective action planning process to support her in acting strategically to increase her situational understanding (Elliott, 1993a) and to bring about change, not only in her department but in confronting staff and student attitudes and challenging the existing culture of the school.

Inquiry as Integral to Professional Practice

Penny's work shows how inquiry is not only integrated but has become integral to her practice; she is a teacher–researcher. She has found ways of collecting evidence and investigating her chosen themes and issues without expending vast amounts of extra time and energy on sophisticated data collection activities, devising creative strategies which fit into her everyday practice as intended in the reflective action planning approach:

> The methods of research, evaluation and quality assurance tend to be dominated by pseudo-objective approaches such as surveying through questionnaires and there is therefore a tendency for inquiry to be seen as a pointless bureaucratic exercise demanded by outsiders who neither know nor care about the real problems experienced by teachers and other professionals. We need instead common-sense methods of inquiry which practitioners can easily build into their routine development work.
>
> (Frost, 1997: 18)

Penny employed a wide range of inquiry techniques in the course of her development work, which are summarized below along with brief comments as to how Penny used them to support her investigations and actions:

- interviews with students, to evaluate the course, review their progress and attitudes and hear their experiences of life in the sixth form;
- interviews with staff, to gain insights into their perceptions and initiate dialogue about school culture;
- consultation with outside agencies contributing to the course, to provide additional information;
- analysis of case study evidence, to enable evaluation of the course in context;
- critical incident analysis (Tripp, 1984) leading to action planning, to address particular problems arising in the course of the development work;
- discussion with critical friends within and outside school, to test ideas and provide an alternative perspective;
- use of literature, to support or challenge argument;
- keeping a professional journal, accounts of observations, interviews, meetings, conversations and feelings to document progress and to use as a basis for reflection, action planning and reporting;
- writing of critical narrative, to give access to interpretations of events and reveal hidden knowledge.

Apart from the interviews with staff and some with students, these are activities which, while systematically planned and carried out, were not discrete episodes of data gathering but were ongoing elements of the inquiry process, feeding into Penny's strategic action to develop the course and raise its status. A high degree of reflexivity was achieved, exploring the interplay of different evidence and perspectives through reflection, writing and discussion.

Reporting, Consultation and Collaboration

While Penny assumed the major responsibility for all the phases of her development work, she became increasingly confident in reporting to different audiences, supported by RAP group workshops and discussions and through the tutorial process. She was convinced of the value of communicating about the work she was involved in, consulting with colleagues within and beyond the school, in order to explore different strategies to confront problematic issues standing in the way of development. She discovered that sometimes it is the relationships *within* school which are harder to develop:

> I have critical friends ... with whom I have regular dialogue sounding out and comparing ideas. It is very different discussing my inquiry with a group of other teachers similarly engaged in their own action research to that of collaborating with colleagues in school. It was not until almost a year into my research that I changed from working virtually alone to working collaboratively with the Head of GNVQ Business. Realizing a united front was needed to campaign for the status and understanding of GNVQ in the school we began to work collaboratively, giving presentations and writing reports ... and managed to start the change process.
>
> (Skoyles, 1998a: 14)

Penny discovered early in her inquiry work the value of listening to her students and involving them in discussion about their own learning, a theme which has emerged increasingly through the discourse within CANTARNET and through its journal, *The Enquirer* (see for example Woods, 1997; Sparke et al., 1998). She reflects:

> I learnt a valuable lesson in realizing the benefit of being able to listen to students' ideas and not take personally students' criticism of the teaching methods I used. Giving students the opportunity to develop their own styles of learning boosted their motivation beyond my expectations.
>
> (Skoyles, 1998a: 11)

Penny went on to involve students in the development process as she initiated and improved the GNVQ course; they 'tested out my theories, sometimes challenged my beliefs' (Skoyles, 1998a: 105). The reflective action planning process, then, has helped Penny to recognize opportunities for consultation and communication and given her the confidence to make use of them through a framework of practical support within the school-based scheme.

Having achieved her master's degree, Penny is still firmly committed to the reflective action planning approach and has become the in-school co-ordinator for her school-based group, continuing to attend meetings and support others in the school who are leading inquiry-based development work and working towards accreditation. She supports the activities of CANTARNET and has published articles in the network journal, *The Enquirer*, to encourage others in reflective practice (Sparke et al., 1998), to demystify the Internet and reveal its value for teacher researchers (Skoyles, 1998b), and to share experience of her own professional journey, which involves both personal professional development and contribution to school development (Skoyles, 1999).

Increasing Teachers' Capacity for 'Change Agentry'

The reflective action planning model was conceived as a process to support teachers in working for change. Penny's experience of using the model as a framework for development work demonstrates that there are a number of elements which have been significant in increasing her agency within the school.

Participation in the School-Based Group Meetings

Discussion of issues in a supportive, constructive, non-hierarchical group helped Penny to find her voice and brought her into contact with other members of staff she would not otherwise have encountered. While her previous experience had been that schools were particularly hierarchical places 'even down to the allocation of chairs in the staffroom …' (unpublished interview data), and she had been physically isolated in a classroom remote from the main school buildings, and socially isolated through having to spend non-contact time in preparation, the group was a major factor in helping her to 'belong' and therefore enabling her to develop her own professional network within the school. She found that she was able to contribute ideas and opinions in discussion with senior colleagues, and this had a major impact on her confidence. Later, the group provided a forum for discussion of problematic issues raised by the development work in hand, giving her supportive but critical feedback on her ideas and dilemmas which she could then feed into her thinking and action planning for further stages of the development work. This too helped to counteract her professional isolation in initiating and following through development work which was far from straightforward.

The Support of the In-School Co-ordinator

It was important in the early stages of her involvement in the scheme that Penny had an in-school tutor or mentor to whom she could turn for advice, guidance and support. This has also emerged as significant in other groups, particularly since tutors who are HEI-based are often peripatetic and can be difficult to contact. As well as guiding her through the accredited framework, this more senior and established member of staff was able to offer insights into the school context and suggestions as to contacts which could usefully be made to enhance the development work. This confidential critical friendship and support again boosted confidence, gave reassurance and helped to widen Penny's sphere of contact. Penny is now able to offer similar support to colleagues involved in the earlier stages of the accredited programme.

Respect for Systematic Inquiry

As outlined above, Penny gathered information and insights systematically as part of the development process, supported by the methodological guidance within the scheme in the form of reading, guidance materials specific to the programme, workshops and discussions during the group meetings and tutorial support for her individual inquiry work. She explains the complexity of the interactive inquiry process as follows:

> To improve one's practice one needs to continually examine and reflect on courses of action to bring about change. This is a skill that I have used throughout my inquiry to analyse strategies used to stimulate and encourage learning ... Action research has made me want to initiate change, has made me critical of the processes used to bring about change and has led me to question my values and beliefs in education.
>
> (Skoyles, 1998a: 105)

The reflective action planning model gives a framework for the collection and analysis of evidence as part of the development process which injects rigour and earns respect in a climate where, as several senior managers pointed out in interview, change is often rushed through and can be planned haphazardly and on the basis of instinct and edict, rather than supported by contextual evidence.

The Requirement to Negotiate, Consult and Report

This emphasis on setting individual teachers' work firmly within the context of school development priorities can sometimes be uncomfortable since it forces them to confront resistance, to acknowledge the wider picture and to deal with problematic issues. Ultimately, it increases agency since the individual has to learn to work strategically within the existing professional networks; in practice, these networks are usually extended further than they might have been as the change agent seeks opportunities for consultation and feedback as part of the inquiry process and develops the confidence to report on progress and outcomes. In developing the GNVQ course, Penny created strategies to change colleagues' attitudes towards her group of less able students; for example, she showed a video of the group in class which demonstrated their engagement with the course and the quality of work they were producing and she also arranged for the group to provide the catering for a staff development day, both of which were probably considerably more effective than making a formal presentation at a staff meeting.

Penny was empowered by the combination of these different elements of the reflective action planning process and the scheme structure, to become a most effective change agent. The culmination of this has been her recognition of her own power to effect change. Her stance is best explained in her own words, with particular reference to the work on the GNVQ course:

> During the two years of developing my skills as an action researcher I have also developed myself as a change agent. The critical dialogue that has taken place with ... colleagues prior to any change has given me the confidence to speak with authority. I have made myself more visible by using my voice and as a reflective practitioner have learnt from these experiences to improve the next action. The changes I have been involved in have influenced the staff's perception of me and becoming GNVQ co-ordinator has improved my professional position within the school. From studying and analysing the issues arising out of my inquiry, I have learnt a lot about myself [and] I am now more aware of the school culture and its effect on bringing about change ...
>
> (Skoyles, 1998a: 100)

Becoming 'Skilled in Change'

Fullan, in his examination of 'change agentry' (1993), argues that 'managing moral purpose and change agentry is at the heart of productive educational change' and that 'the building block is the moral purpose of the individual teacher' since the individual can have a stronger leverage for change (1993: 8–10). Penny Skoyles's story illustrates graphically Fullan's ideas about change agentry which he defines as 'being self-conscious about the nature of change and the change process'. Through reflective action planning, Penny has become 'skilled in change':

> appreciative of its semi-unpredictable and volatile character ... explicitly concerned with the pursuit of ideas and competencies for coping with and influencing more and more aspects of the process towards some desired set of ends.
>
> (Fullan, 1993: 12)

As we discussed with Andrew's story in the previous chapter, Penny's professional journey has also resulted in her coming to embody the four core capacities which Fullan believes are needed to build teachers' overall capacity for change agentry. *Personal vision building* involves exploring and reaching a greater understanding of purpose as an educator. Fullan believes that 'personal vision in teaching is too often implicit and dormant' (1993: 13) and that it needs to be unlocked so that teachers are able to conceptualize their roles at a higher level, as Penny has increasingly been able to do at each stage of her development work.

Inquiry fuels ideas about personal purpose by uncovering ideas, information and issues through persistent questioning, becoming 'the engine of vitality and self-renewal' (Pascale, in Fullan 1993: 15). This enables teachers to adjust their mental maps to new territory as a lifelong process; essential to change agentry. Thus Penny concludes her five years with a conviction that her learning will continue and a vision of the school as a learning community, intending to contribute herself to the changing culture by drawing colleagues into the inquiry process:

> I hope that through this work, which obviously does not stop with the completion of this dissertation, I can continue to make small but significant steps, to update and improve the culture of the school, to influence the staff to become more collaborative and reflective in their practice, to be flexible and more responsive to the positive outcomes of change and the development of their professional learning, creating a learning community in which all the occupants strive for improvement and success.
>
> (Skoyles, 1998a:110)

Mastery involves clarifying what is important, through inquiry and expression of personal vision, and then learning to see it more clearly (Fullan 1993: 16). It is about taking more effective action towards results, which requires continuing professional learning. One theme emerging strongly in Penny's story, that of increasing confidence, is highlighted by Fullan (after Rozenholtz, 1989) as a key aspect of mastery:

> The more accustomed one becomes at dealing with the unknown, the more one understands that creative breakthroughs are always preceded by periods of cloudy thinking, confusion, exploration, trial and stress; followed by periods of excitement and growing confidence as one pursues purposeful change, or copes with unwanted change.
>
> (Fullan, 1993: 17)

The self-confidence which develops with self-awareness, including understanding personal limitations and weaknesses, enables teachers to manage the change process more realistically and effectively, to 'behave their way into new ideas and skills, not think their way into them' (Fullan, 1993: 15).

Collaboration is the final capacity which Fullan believes is essential to personal learning. Penny places unquestionable importance on the development of professional relationships and networks to support her development work. We have seen the ways in which the reflective action planning model explicitly encourages this through the activities of the school-based group and the wider network, and through emphasizing negotiation, reporting, consultation and collaboration throughout the process.

Conclusion

Penny and others have found that the boundaries of the award-bearing aspect of the programme are transcended as a reflective and investigative approach becomes a professional way of life; inquiry does not end with the achievement of an academic award. It helps teachers to acknowledge and understand the interrelationships and complexities of educational change in relation to the individual professional context, and supports them in taking action. It is not simply a matter of competence, efficiency, possession of knowledge and development of technique, but involves 'pleasure, passion, creativity, challenge and joy' (Hargreaves, 1998: 110), and above all, *care for children*, whatever the national and institutional context, whatever the latest initiative, whatever the media message this week. In an investigation into why students wanted to become teachers, Fullan found that most frequently mentioned theme was that of wanting to make a difference to children's lives (1993: 10). Penny includes in her master's dissertation a vignette which reveals that her core values echo this; the development of the GNVQ course and the impact on attitudes within the school has had a life-changing effect on her students. Her writing demonstrates the interplay between reflection, analysis and action with moral purpose which characterizes her approach as an experienced teacher–researcher.

Jason

> Jason was a particular challenge. I had stuck to my plan to treat him as though I had not taught him recently, but his behaviour at times was unacceptable. He was very outspoken, and often over-familiar with me. He tended to make sarcastic remarks to members of the group, leading to arguments; an agreed set of rules helped to resolve this problem. I soon realized part of Jason's behaviour was because he had to compensate for the fact that he had a Learning Support Assistant (LSA) helping him. The LSA was a motherly figure who continually called him 'dear' and he was embarrassed by this, although he realized he needed her assistance. A quiet word with the LSA helped, and arranging for him to be away from the group with his LSA for designated lessons helped with his

concentration and performance. Jason was at times very immature but would shine in situations where he was given a role, for example when we had visiting speakers it was his job to arrange the room and be in charge of setting up the video or tape recorder. Gradually his self-esteem grew and I received comments from visitors about his caring nature, with one speaker actually indicating that if he wanted further training her company would definitely take him on. Jason's work experience reports came back with glowing comments on how helpful and enthusiastic he had been, willing to turn his hand to any task set. Jason very gradually became a reformed character for me; he was struggling with his work at times, but he was becoming critically aware of his capabilities and had developed himself personally, discovering the important values of self-confidence and assertiveness ... this enabled his learning to progress. To his credit, Jason passed three end of unit tests, he was able to have a reader for these multiple choice questions. Several students had to retake these exams so again his morale was boosted as he had passed them first time. He left school, having the choice of two jobs, with training, offered by his work placements ...

(Skoyles, 1998a: 73)

At the end of Penny's account of her development work, we are left not with the conclusions of her 'research findings' but with a passionate statement of vision and moral purpose which is true to the values she began to articulate at the start of her five-year journey:

There is much work for teachers to do, we all now need to find the strength to navigate imposed reforms and rekindle the passion that stimulates children to be enthusiastic about learning.

(Skoyles, 1998a: 111)

Penny's story shows that the reflective action planning process empowers individual teachers to challenge their own thinking and increases their capacity to focus their energy and commitment into leading effective and appropriate change which they know will improve the educational experiences and opportunities for their students.

9 Developing Teacher Professionalism Through Networking

The CANTARNET Story

The first time attendee at a principals' centre conference arrives promptly at the beginning of the second day without having had a chance to first consult the programme. Twenty to thirty people are drinking coffee, eating pastries, and milling comfortably between four or five conversation groups scattered throughout the lounge area. After thirty minutes of good talk on an issue of special interest to her, the newcomer looks at her watch and feels guilty: 'But what are we supposed to be doing?' she asks the woman next to her. '*This*', she is quickly assured.

(Lieberman and Grolnick, 1996: 1)

In recent years, teacher networks have been portrayed, in the American school improvement literature at least, as part of the 'new professionalism' (McLaughlin, 1997) although many of the examples used actually date from the 1970s; for example, McLaughlin cites the National Writing Project funded in 1974, and Lieberman and Grolnick (1996) cite the work of Allen Parker (1977) and Goodlad (1977) in documenting the development of teacher networks. In Britain too we have seen manifestations of teacher networking, for example, linked to the Schools Council curriculum projects of the 1960s and 1970s. There has always been a considerable degree of subject-related networking fostered by the subject associations and local education authority (LEA) inspectors and advisors and, in the 1980s, networking was fostered by TVEI (the Technical and Vocational Education Initiative). However, it was relatively uncommon for networking to be an explicit goal. A notable exception is CARN (Collaborative Action Research Network) established in 1976 specifically to facilitate teachers' networking on a worldwide basis although, as its founder reports, the organization has increasingly become less a network of teachers and more a network of higher education academics (Elliott, 1996b). Networking is integral to the very nature of action research in that it necessarily involves individuals and groups working within particular contexts and on specific cases. Therefore, participants need to gain access to other cases and engage in critical friendship in order to challenge their own perspectives and practices. Action research implies a shift from 'didactics' to 'dialectics' in professional development pedagogy (Bell, 1989).

123

The revival of interest in networking can be seen as part of a fundamental global movement which the sociologist Manuel Castells calls 'information-alism': 'In the new informational mode of development the source of productivity lies in the technology of knowledge generation, information processing and symbol communication' (Castells, 1996: 17). What is most interesting about Castells's account is the idea that improvements in the technology of information processing help to shape the nature of knowledge generation itself and this clearly spotlights the use of the Internet and related technologies in the field of professional networks. The question is not whether the rapid technological developments driven by the restructuring of capitalism since the 1980s are helping to shape the nature of teacher networking behaviours; it is patently clear that they are; rather the question is whether they are shaping the fundamental nature of the professional discourse engaged in and whether this development is likely to be of benefit to the profession and ultimately to the education of young people in our schools.

In this chapter, we explore networking by reflecting on the development of CANTARNET (Canterbury Action Research Network), a regional network built around the reflective action planning groups established in a large number of Kent secondary schools. We consider the nature of the activities associated with the network and the way in which these activities can enhance inquiry-based development work in schools, provide a forum for discussion about teaching and learning and support the continuing professional development of teachers. We also raise questions about power, politics and ownership. Finally, we consider the future for such activities within the national context, focusing in particular on the role of information and communications technology as a medium for professional dialogue. Clearly the potential is increasing as new technologies present greater and more sophisticated possibilities for professional networking, but we need to be prepared to address a range of issues that will inevitably arise. CANTARNET has provided a great deal of support, inspiration and opportunity for sharing and exploring ideas but there are a number of dangers and difficulties which need to be considered.

A Rationale for Establishing a Network

When the first proposals were made to pilot a school-based, award-bearing professional development/school improvement scheme (see Chapter 2), sceptics raised a number of issues about the siting of a programme within a single school. They pointed to the danger that insularity, complacency and self-satisfaction might be encouraged; it was feared quite reasonably perhaps that the pragmatist philosophy of the programme might lead to what Bridges has called 'perceptual and conceptual myopia' (1996: 254). However, it was defended on the grounds that, because it is an academic programme leading to a recognized award, it is bound to involve critical scrutiny of the particular ideas and practices in the local setting together with the examination of alternative perspectives through the literature. Barnett (1990) argues that the purpose of higher education is to enable students to achieve intellectual independence through an emancipatory process which liberates them from their particular concerns and specialisms. At the beginning of this project, we took seriously our responsibility to ensure that participants are drawn into critical debate about practice and to provide both support and challenge for systematic inquiry. Subsequently, it became clear that the scheme needed a networking dimension to extend and enrich the discourse.

In the pilot project, our strategies were limited to putting forward suggestions that participants should ask the school to allow them time to visit other schools, and that participants should see literature as not simply 'theory' but as sources of accounts of practice elsewhere. In promoting the idea of such networking we tended to use a sub-heading from Fullan's 'Change Forces' as a slogan: 'Ideas Are Out There' (1993: 85), but Fullan's discussion of networking tended to concentrate on the idea of schools as institutions participating in networks and alliances in the context of large scale educational reform rather than teachers networking with other teachers as individuals. There are many good accounts of such networks on either side of the Atlantic providing *schools* with opportunities to learn from each other (for example Bridges and Husbands, 1996; Lieberman and Grolnick, 1996; Lieberman and McLaughlin, 1992). We had direct experience of schools collaborating and networking through local partnerships, for example under the TVEI umbrella and, later, for the purposes of initial teacher education. However, these models did not tell us a great deal about networking arrangements for individual teachers.

At the beginning, we tried to encourage teachers participating in the scheme to make contact with other teachers who had experience of whatever the practical concern might be and to visit their schools or correspond with them. As more schools joined the scheme, we were in a position to identify common concerns for teachers in our groups on an *ad hoc* basis. Nevertheless, we were forced to admit that participants were not experiencing routinely the enrichment of working with colleagues drawn from a wide range of schools in the region, as would be the case with a more traditional university-based masters course. We were becoming increasingly aware that the teachers in our groups were missing out on the considerable benefit to be had from contrasting practice and applying alternative perspectives directly through personal contact with colleagues in other schools.

Within our own research group (the ESACS Project; see Chapter 5), we noted the significance of the nature of the discourse through which we planned our collaborative work. We tape recorded our discussions and reflected self-consciously on the discursive process; we confronted issues to do with hierarchy and status and concluded that professional discourse is most likely to become truly critical when certain conditions prevail. Our analysis told us that good professional discourse has the sort of features set out in Figure 9.1 below.

125

Figure 9.1

Features of Good Professional Discourse

- expression of solidarity
- recognition of correspondence
- comparison of experience
- application of a variety of perspectives
- application of a range of expertise
- question posing
- demand for clarification
- discussion of alternative strategies
- validation of interpretation
- challenging of interpretation
- exploration of values

Our views about the purposes and the processes of networking were shaped by this exploration.

A Proposal to Develop a Local Network

The rationale for the establishment of CANTARNET was that its members could not only be informed about development work in other schools but could also make personal contact with teachers in schools within easy reach. Such knowledge and contacts had become scarce and precious commodities since LEA support had diminished. In addition, access to other national and international networks such as CARN would provide network members with information, ideas and support from across the world.

The Aims of CANTARNET

According to McLaughlin (1997), teacher networks have been formed variously around particular reform strategies, geographical areas, specific topics and subject areas. The CANTARNET proposal clearly suggested no such themes, common foci or subjects, but can be seen instead as arising from the desire to provide a framework within which participants in our scheme could extend and enrich beyond the school the critical discourse which appeared to be flourishing within the RAP groups.

The essential elements of the proposal were:

- one day conferences would be held once each term;
- a journal would be published once per term featuring teachers' accounts of their development work;

- a 'contacts list' would be assembled, providing an outline of participants' development work and indicating whether they would have a report available, be interested in further collaboration, or be willing to make a presentation;
- a website including the journal, the 'contacts list' and links to other sites would be established;
- set-up affiliation to CARN would involve the in-school co-ordinator becoming a member.

The proposal also included the provision of access to the HEI's library catalogue via a website link.

CANTARNET was launched with an inaugural conference on 4th May 1996, at which the first edition of the journal, *The Enquirer*, was published. Our conviction about the need for this development was expressed in the editorial of the first edition of the journal and encapsulated our hopes and intentions:

> So, what I believe we need is a live network which puts teachers in touch with each other and encourages them to communicate with each other about areas of common interest. We also need more critical debate about the curriculum at the local level. In the past few years we have developed school-based action research groups within which there is a tremendous level of critical discussion and some excellent inquiry but ... the discourse needs to be extended by reaching out firstly to other groups and individuals in the area, and then beyond to established networks in the UK and abroad.
>
> (Frost, 1996a: 1)

The Ownership of Networks

The initiative arose out of the dialogue between a small group of mostly part-time tutors who were encouraged by the teachers in the RAP groups who were enthusiastic about the idea of meeting teachers from other groups and learning about practice in other schools. The decision was subsequently validated in the sense that the conferences have been attended by between forty and sixty teachers on each occasion, and the journal has been supported by contributions from members of the network.

However, given that the overall aim was to facilitate teachers' own networking activity, it might be argued that procedures ought to have been established for the governance of the network to ensure that it was managed in the interests of the members. Elliott's narrative about similar issues in the operation of CARN is instructive: according to him, CARN had no organization beyond a list of members circulated by himself as the founder of the network (Elliott, 1996b). Later, a debate about the issue of ownership led to a bid on the part of teacher members to draw up a constitution and to establish a representative steering group but, as the Co-ordinators' report to the annual conference in 1996 made clear, no such formal constitution was ever written and CARN ultimately became largely a network of teacher educators and similar academics. So far, there has been no suggestion that CANTARNET needs a constitution and the post-conference evaluations continue to suggest that those who attend are finding the events satisfying. However, we remain concerned about questions of leadership and ownership and whether the long-term health of the network will be affected by such issues.

Facilitating Networking through Conferences

The tension between the mobilization of resources for didactics and the management of spaces for dialectics exists in almost any in-service teacher education scenario. There is a tendency to see the provision of highly structured and focused specialist input as being of higher priority and thus requiring more thought and ingenuity than the provision of a framework for dialogue. However, we have found both aspects equally important and challenging. Our conferences were organized with the following aims in mind:

- to stimulate and challenge with a good keynote input from a person who has published and would be name familiar to participants;
- to provide formal sessions for structured discussion in which participants could share information, contrast experiences and provide each other with psychological support;
- to provide space for informal contact and opportunities for discussion in which participants could share information, contrast experiences, provide each other with psychological support;
- to provide information and coaching on specific skills such as library searching and using the computer to access the Internet;
- to provide an opportunity to examine and buy books and to use the library;
- to provide opportunities for participants to make arrangements for further networking beyond the conference.

It was clear from our evaluations of the conferences that opportunities for discussion were highly valued, but that the informal opportunities were either less well managed or participants were less able to take advantage of them. We had discussed the idea of providing space for people to meet and talk to each other, and also providing name badges and a displayed list of participants and an outline of their development work, within a central meeting place with coffee and biscuits. We eventually realized that people often needed personal introductions, so we undertook to mingle with the crowd and introduce participants to each other. The evaluation sheets consistently told us that participants would welcome more time to share or discuss their concerns in a more structured session, but they also told us that keynote speakers are stimulating and thought-provoking. Clearly, we needed to maintain the balance between input and networking opportunities.

It is difficult to determine the extent to which the last aim on the list above – to provide opportunities for participants to make arrangements for further networking – is being fulfilled. At all the conferences, participants are to be seen huddled in corners not only discussing areas of common concern but also exchanging telephone numbers and making arrangements for further contact. We were able to provide further support for this activity by displaying the database of participants' work prominently in the central space for coffee, registration and permissible milling, and this evolved into a contacts list which is published both at conferences and on the Internet. We have some anecdotal evidence that incidents of networking between participants from different schools are on the increase; although it is impossible to quantify this, the conferences appear to be an important focus for professional dialogue which helps to strengthen contact between colleagues from different schools.

Publishing Teachers' Work through a Network Journal

The first issue of *The Enquirer*, the network journal, was launched at CANTARNET's inaugural conference and has been published two or three times a year since then. We knew that most of the participants in the scheme were hard-pressed to produce the material vital for the implementation of their professional action plans, and often tended to delay the documentation of their development work because of the chronic shortage of time. It is hardly surprising therefore that participants said that they did not have the time to write additional material for *The Enquirer*. Writing is a difficult and time-consuming task which also demands a considerable degree of confidence. In the light of this, we tried to make it easy for teachers to contribute. In addition, we assumed that the journal would lack impact unless the process was direct and immediate, in contrast to our experience of the refereed journals where an inordinate amount of time could pass between a paper being submitted and it appearing in print. For *The Enquirer*, the whole process from submission to publishing is a matter of a few weeks. This means, of course, that the whole business of commenting on manuscripts and amending them has to be cut short. In practice, the editing has been fast and could in some cases be described as impertinent; it has to be admitted that it relies on a great deal of trust. In more recent issues, tutors have been involved in an intermediate role to offer support and comment before contributions are submitted which makes the prospect of publication more possible and approachable for many. Even so, it is questionable whether authors would always have the confidence to challenge the editor's judgements. There is always the danger that a contributor's views are misrepresented by a slip of the editorial pen or that changing an author's prose undermines self-esteem leading to ill feeling.

At the time of writing, the journal continues to be produced very rapidly, and although it has been suggested by some that there should be an editorial panel, there seems to be little support for the idea. Our survey of the views of the membership indicates that what is of most value is the immediacy of the response coupled with the small scale and local focus of the activity. However, what has emerged as a quite different approach to editorial control is the idea of the editorial function passing from one school to another, so that the RAP group receives contributions from across the network and then makes editorial decisions as a group. Early indications are that this gives each group in turn a powerful sense of ownership of the journal as well as an enhanced sense of commitment to the network as a whole.

Contributions to the Journal

A recurring issue has concerned the nature and authorship of contributions to the journal. Prior to the publication of the first issue, all participants in RAP groups had been invited to contribute either case studies extracted from the work they had already produced or any other item that they thought would be interesting or provocative.

Contributions by teachers were not dominant in this first issue. However, the balance did improve: in the second issue there were eight papers by teachers and two by academics, and in the third issue there were nine contributions from teachers and no papers by academics except the editorial. The balance of contributions has fluctuated comfortably after this, and so far there has always been sufficient material for the journal, due largely to the commitment of tutors within the scheme who elicit material through approaching individuals with suggestions and encouragement as to how they might adapt and publish existing writing.

Our investigations over the first few issues of the journal clearly indicated that readers were generally pleased to be able to access accounts of other teachers' development work as well as 'academic' research or argument, which they tended to find less readable or accessible. Most of the papers published contained some kind of narrative about the author's inquiry-led school improvement work; for example, Sue Deans (1997) wrote about her work developing Media Education in a climate increasingly hostile to that subject, and Geoff Wells (1997) wrote about managing change in the context of the development of the use of the Internet by colleagues in his school. However, quite a number of CANTARNET members said that they did not have enough time to read the journal, and there was also a concern that some of the papers were less appealing than they might be because they were not written with this particular medium in mind.

This suggests an interesting dilemma: we were able eventually to limit publication to teachers' papers, but the style of many of these papers remained distinctly academic, that is to say, rather precise and impersonal, rather long and laboured, supported with references to literature and so on. This problem cannot be attributed to the system of academic refereeing since we have had no such policy; rather, the explanation lies in the fact that most of these papers were written in the first instance for an academic audience. Of course, participants would all have produced a range of different kinds of papers for their portfolios, but these items are not easily represented in a publishable form and so, particularly in the early issues of the journal, we found that teachers' papers tend to be abridged versions of parts of their dissertations. More recently, articles have tended to be written specifically for the journal so it could be said to have become less theory and literature laden and has less academic argument. Our research suggests that in this form the articles are more readable, but at the same time they do contribute to the body of case study knowledge and to the ongoing dialogue of the network. The following extract from an *Enquirer* editorial gives a flavour of the range and content of the journal.

We are delighted that in this issue the majority of the articles are written by teacher members of CANTARNET so that the focus remains very much on schools, classrooms and teachers' professional concerns. There is a practical emphasis and an immediacy in the writing which challenges us to re-examine our practice, not only in terms of considering the way we act but also in digging deeper to explore the values and motives underlying what we do ... Andrew Wright's painful experiences of inappropriate INSET offer a salutary lesson for those who aspire to the role of self-appointed experts, and lead us to question the ways in which effective professional learning is best supported ... Jill Oliphant-Robertson allows her Yr. 9 students to express in their own words what they have learnt from their participation in a 'Values Forum' but also feels that she herself has learnt alongside them. Through some recent work on the identification and analysis of critical incidents (Tripp, 1984), Penny Skoyles and Jon Sparke uncover the meanings and implications behind everyday classroom events. This has not only given them new insights as classroom teachers but has also demonstrated, through group discussion, the power and value of reflections shared ... April 30th 1998 was an important day for CANTARNET as a group of representatives from across the network met with Michael Barber to share concerns and gain a central perspective of educational change. Gary Holden reports on this meeting and it is encouraging to see a note from Michael Barber in response; we hope that this has opened a channel of communication for the future. Meanwhile, Penny Skoyles has acquired a world-wide perspective through her exploration of the Internet and is now so committed to its value in supporting her practice and her research that the rest of her family find themselves excluded! Her article will convince both the terri-fied and the cynical, while old hands might like to check they have bookmarked her list of useful websites. Diana MacAdie questions whether her experience on a work placement with a salad packaging firm is being used effectively back in school and invites ideas and comments, particularly from those who have had similar encounters with the world beyond the classroom ... While much of the writing in this issue is eminently practical, offering ideas and strategies which are directly applicable, prepare also to be inspired. In particular, Tom Hedger's article, in which he explores his personal professional values as an art teacher, reminds us that teaching is 'emotional work'; it is not simply a matter of competence, efficiency, possession of knowledge and development of technique, but involves 'pleasure, passion, creativity, challenge and joy' (Hargreaves, 1997, p.110), and above all, care for children. Collectively, the writing in this and previous editions of 'The Enquirer' is a refreshing anti-dote to the depressing national caricature of the profession which we seem to encounter daily. It testifies to the fact that passion and creativity have not been completely submerged under mounting paperwork or progressively dulled by disillusionment. We are reminded throughout of the core purpose of our individual and collaborative enquiry, reflection and action, which is clearly focused on children and their learning.

(Durrant, 1998)

Networking through the Internet

From the outset, the intention was that the Internet would be used to support networking within CANTARNET so that it could be continual rather than relying on discrete events. It was proposed that this would be done in the following ways:

1   *The Enquirer* would be published on the Internet so that it would consti-tute an archive of papers which would obviously be an increasingly rich resource over time. Articles could easily be reproduced by downloading and printing, and they could become a focus for global networking.
2   The contacts list would be continuously updated and would facilitate networking on local, national and international levels. By listing individ-uals' e-mail addresses as 'hot links', a person interested in the development work they are reading about would only need to click on the individual's name in order to send them an e-mail message.
3   The 'Dialogue Box', which is an integral part of *The Enquirer*, would enable participants and anyone accessing the website to comment on what they had read in the journal or to raise any other issues for debate.

Use of the 'on-line' version of *The Enquirer* was slow at first; we know that there were approximately twenty 'visits' to the website in both September and October 1998, and this increased dramatically to sixty 'visits' in November. At the time of writing the archive consists of approximately sixty case studies. When the contacts list was first published, only a handful of network members had been able to supply e-mail addresses with which to achieve the 'hot links'. This was easily attributed to the lack of access to computers connected to the Internet, together with the lack of confidence and expertise to use it. However, it is assumed that the current emphasis on ICT training and web-based learning for teachers should soon have an impact in this respect. The CANTARNET conferences have consistently included a workshop on the use of the Internet and evaluations indicate that they have been successful as events. More recently we have begun to experiment with the idea of 'learning forums' which are web-based conferences focused on a particular theme, 'chaired' or moderated and set within a limited time frame. A conference has a number of threads, and there are both open forums and ones which are limited to a pre-arranged list of participants. The experiment is ongoing.

Meanwhile, the Prime Minister himself put his name to the government's attempt to offer leadership in this area when, in October 1997, he wrote the foreword to the consultation document: 'Connecting the Learning Society: National Grid for Learning' (DfEE, 1997a). His statement concluded with these words:

> By 2002, all schools will be connected to the superhighway, free of charge; half a million teachers will be trained; and our children will be leaving school IT-literate, having been able to exploit the best that technology can offer. We believe this strategy will be good for our children and our companies.

In November 1998, the National Grid for Learning was launched. The 'Grid' was defined as:

> A way of finding and using on-line learning and teaching materials. A mosaic of inter-connecting networks and education services based on the Internet which will support teaching, learning, training and administration in schools, colleges, universities, libraries, the workplace and homes.
>
> (DfEE, 1997a)

Responses to the consultation indicated widespread support although the DfEE's analysis was of the responses they received; 90 per cent of responses were very supportive of the initiative while only 1 per cent was wholly negative. This is hardly surprising, of course, since the act of reading the consultation document and making a response is a fairly good indicator of having some commitment to the enterprise in the first place. The analysis of responses (DfEE, 1998) revealed, again unsurprisingly, that the majority of respondents (80 per cent) emphasized the need to develop their expertise and confidence and (70 per cent) the need to gain access to computers outside of the normal teaching hours. A large proportion of respondents (60 per cent) said that it is important to build on current local initiatives, although it would have been useful to know more about what benefits teachers currently derive from these. Our experience in discussing these issues within RAP groups is that teachers can only develop their expertise when they have access to computers outside of teaching time so that they can explore the technology and pursue their own particular needs and interests through it. It is hoped that the plummeting price of personal computers coupled with the government's recent initiative to subsidize teachers' purchases of laptop computers will go some way to addressing this problem.

Coupling Teacher Networks to the National Policy Train

The question of the link between local initiatives and national policy is an extremely important one for CANTARNET. Our own website has always included links to other useful sites such as the DfEE Homepage, The Standards Site, TeacherNet UK, The Virtual Teachers Centre, The Times Educational Supplement Online and so on. However a recent search of the National Grid for Learning reveals that this service is not reciprocal and the supposedly all-embracing Standards Site does not offer links to CANTARNET. Perhaps in time the mysterious powers behind 'the Grid' will be persuaded to provide links to local sites in order to encourage teachers and schools to learn from each other. Such a move would certainly be in keeping with the DfEE's current enthusiasm for 'Beacon Schools' and the like (TES, 1998).

One aspect of our concern about these developments is the extent to which state-sponsored networks can actually facilitate teachers' own networking activity, and, related to this is the concern that, if such networks achieve a monopoly, then the impact of the state on educational discourse could become even more hegemonic than it is at present. Firestone and Pennell (1997) put it thus:

> there is a potential tension in using networks as part of a state strategy for educational reform. The autonomy and opportunity for leadership that networks offer teachers (Lieberman and McLaughlin, 1992) appear to contribute directly to their effectiveness. It is not at all clear that these features can be maintained when networks are brought into the orbit of state government.
>
> (Firestone and Pennell, 1997: 238)

They adopt a position which is critical of the view that networks are appropriate vehicles for the establishment of standards and means of accountability in the context of national reform agendas. The key issue is whether the professional knowledge created through such networking activities is constructed collectively by the members of the network or simply delivered by conference organizers and workshop leaders. For us, the question is whether CANTARNET is helping to generate knowledge in a dialectical way, through mutual discussion set in the local context, or whether it might be drifting towards a more didactic approach in which 'right thinking' emanating from the DfEE is simply disseminated and reinforced.

Firestone and Pennell's conclusions from only two case studies of American teacher networks suggest that 'capacity building networks contribute more directly to teacher learning, motivation, and empowerment than do policy-supporting networks' (1997: 263). They also conclude that a great range of teachers are attracted to networks if they use a mix of 'constructivist and directive activities'. Thus they are not against state-sponsored networks, provided that they are of the constructivist sort.

Issues for Future Debate and Research

At this critical juncture, there are major issues about the future of CANTARNET and about teacher networks in general. Some of these issues are practical and some are more fundamentally concerned with the nature of civil society. The practical issues are as follows:

(a) There is the question of whether teachers can achieve the necessary expertise and access to the technology to enable them to use the Internet for networking purposes. These are inextricably linked if we accept that the only effective way to learn how to use a computer is to have more or less unrestricted access to it.

(b) There is the question of the role of personal contact and how websites and other electronically based projects can facilitate teachers in their attempts to learn from and with each other through discussion in person, school visits and collaborative work.

(c) There is the question of the design of real time conferences and the extent to which they can facilitate teachers' own networking activity as well as provide information and stimulation.

(d) There is the question of the role of publication of teachers' case studies with all that implies about generalizability or relateability (Bassey, 1995) and intelligibility/readability in terms of both style and length.

The more fundamental issues are concerned with the impact of information technologies, and their use by reforming governments, on the nature of civil society. Arguably, networks such as CANTARNET are organizations which play a small part in enabling people to engage in active citizenship. Ranson et al., for example, argue that what is required is a new vision of the public domain in which 'co-operative action grows out of the capacity of the public domain to generate an orientation to communicative rationality' (1997: 121). Here they are drawing on Habermas's (1981) theory of communicative action in which knowledge is neither objectified nor assumed to reside in the separate minds, the subjective realities, of individuals, but rather can be seen to be an ongoing stream created and recreated out of argument, reflexivity and association. Clearly, the way that discursive practices are shaped has critical implications for the nature of the public domain, and there can be no doubt that acts of leadership and facilitation with regard to information flow, analysis and debate within networks supported by the Internet need to be scrutinized closely to ensure that teachers' capacity for professional judgement and their agency as individuals is enhanced rather than diminished.

There are those who would say that, because professional discourse is being hijacked by the state and networks are in danger of being commandeered in support of national priorities, we must exploit the Internet and other networking strategies to engage in a global debate about practice (Elliott, 1998b). It is ironic perhaps that we are hearing arguments about the usefulness of avoiding the limitations of the national context both from the action research community and from the school effectiveness community (DfEE, 1997b) which would almost certainly see themselves as being at opposite ends of the spectrum.

Finally, there is the question of the role of CANTARNET in providing a forum within which teachers' voices can be heard. Our network is one which brings together teachers who have demonstrated an interest in action research of one sort or another but, as Ivor Goodson has pointed out, there is difficulty in the expectation that the sole focus of teachers' critical scrutiny should be their own practice. Goodson sought to move beyond the albeit laudable notions of 'teacher as researcher' and 'action research' when he said:

> I am worried about a collaborative mode of research which seeks to give full equality and stature to the teacher, but which employs as its initial and predominant focus the practice of the teacher. It is, I believe, a profoundly unpromising point of entry from which to promote a collaborative enterprise.
>
> (Goodson, 1992: 113)

There would seem to be something inequitable about a set of arrangements which had teachers evaluating their own performance as teachers and as managers of change without including the facility to articulate critiques of policy and practice more widely. The CANTARNET conferences provide an opportunity for teachers to speak critically about practices within their own schools in the way that traditional in-service courses have always done. *The Enquirer* journal may appear to offer such an opportunity, but in practice our contributors are naturally constrained by the need to protect the reputations of their schools in the present market-led climate (Bridges and Husbands, 1996). However, CANTARNET can also provide a framework within which teachers' voices can be articulated in a collective way. For example, a CANTARNET delegation visited the DfEE to see Michael Barber, the chair of the government's Standards and Effectiveness Unit, to discuss a number of issues which had been identified at one of the termly conferences (Holden, 1998). The event may seem to be a relatively minor one as political acts go, but when compared to the situation in which individual teachers write critical analyses in dissertations which are read by their university tutors and then confined to the college library and in many cases to a cupboard in the HEI's department of education, it takes on considerable significance.

The delegation to the DfEE arose out of a creative approach to the framing of discussions at the conferences. The main aim was still to facilitate networking. However, the success of the activity has led to the question of the extent to which teacher networks should seek to play a fuller part in the democratic process, acting as pressure groups or at least as representative bodies which can expect to be consulted by agencies of government on relevant matters of policy.

So what next for the network? Our experiment with electronic communications continues with the setting up of a web-based 'learning forum', in addition to the already established website. The idea here is that each term a new topic for debate will be 'posted' on the web-board and participants invited to respond both to the initial stimulus and to each other. We hope this will allow teachers to 'network' at a distance from each other, not in order to replace the face to face contact the conference provides, but to supplement it.

We have also given considerable thought to the role of the journal, and we decided to place responsibility for editing *The Enquirer* with the school-based groups themselves on a rotational basis. The St John's RAP group volunteered to try this for the first time and in their editorial, wrote:

Working on a Change Gang

It is 5.30 in the afternoon. It has been a long day. There are ten of us sitting around a large table in a classroom writing this editorial. Like many classrooms in many schools, it could do with a lick of paint. One or two of the ceiling tiles are missing, and the door doesn't close properly. In the corridors and classrooms outside, cleaners vacuum, mop and polish to get the school ready for tomorrow.

These aren't the best conditions for clear-headed reflection or committed debate. And yet that's exactly what's happening. For the last 90 minutes we have been reading, discussing, arguing, and laughing; we've consumed a pot of coffee and a plate of sandwiches and we're just about to start on

137

the jaffa cakes. We feel strangely refreshed, strengthened. When it's time to go, a few of us will linger in the car park to continue the conversation in the gathering gloom as the caretaker bolts the door behind us ...

The St John's group is now in its sixth year. There are currently 11 participants in the group and 16 teachers have achieved some kind of award during those six years. But more than that, we have come to see ourselves as change agents, working with the culture and values of the school to improve teaching and learning. Not a chain gang then, toiling in the dark for something we can't see, but a change gang, committed to continuous improvement and teacher empowerment.

How have we approached the task of editing the last edition of the Enquirer this century? It's quite a responsibility. We know how valuable we find this termly journal for enabling us to catch up on what colleagues in other schools are doing, to pick up a few tips, and for providing a little food for thought, perhaps even the odd moment of controversy.

We think we have carried out our editorial role in the same spirit of collaborative inquiry that informs our own development work. We have all contributed something; we have invited all participants in the scheme to send articles and we have tried above all to preserve the core values of the Enquirer as a forum for debate and a meeting place for diverse voices, including those of the young people we teach.

(*The Enquirer*, 1999)

10 Teachers 'Making a Difference'

The Question of Impact

The RAP scheme is in essence a school improvement initiative, in that it aims to increase pupils' academic achievement by encouraging teachers to take a systematic, sustained and active approach to change. Fullan and Hargreaves (1992) point out that the key success indicator of any innovatory programme is the extent to which teachers' classroom practice is changed. They draw a distinction between large-scale top-down innovations that demand rapid, radical changes in practice and small-scale, school-initiated, collaborative attempts to work on specific areas of practice. The former have a poor record of success, while the long-term effects of the latter approach appear to be more long lasting and become more deep-rooted within the culture of the school.

Successful schools, argue Hillman and Stoll (1994), 'depend on people … understanding the school's culture and developing it in such a way that supports the process of change' (Hillman and Stoll, 1994: 3). This accurately echoes the ideas underlying the RAP scheme. Individuals are invited to take on the role of change agents in their school, collaborating with other professionals in development activities, and to report on these activities both to audiences within the school, and, via a portfolio of evidence, for accreditation from the HEI. The approach to change is therefore both individual and institutional.

In Chapters 1 and 2, we made it clear that the RAP scheme was seen by its instigators as an antidote to the kind of INSET that is characterized by low levels of relevance and impact. The aims of the pilot project were couched in terms of professional and school development but the statement on the leaflet inviting teachers to take part said quite directly that such development work 'will enhance the quality of learning experienced by students at St Andrew's School'. As the scheme has grown, this assumption, that teacher-led development work will lead to enhanced pupil learning, has been shared comfortably between both group leaders and participants, and it is only quite recently that the question of the link between development work and pupils' learning has become such a challenging one within our network. The school effectiveness discourse has, of course, penetrated our discussions more and more as it poses the challenging question, 'how do you know that this development work will increase pupil learning?' Through the pages of *The Enquirer* and at the CANTARNET conferences we have heard the expression of views which urge network members to move beyond 'outmoded notions of professional autonomy' (Nixon, 1996: 1) and to look for evidence that their professional development is 'making a difference to what and how well students are learning' (Learmonth, 1997: 14).

A particular and forceful challenge comes from the TTA, the body given responsibility for the distribution of funding for teachers' CPD. Since 1998 providers of CPD programmes must ensure that their courses and projects 'have a demonstrable impact on raising standards in schools' in order to continue to be funded by the TTA (TTA, 1998).

So, for a number of reasons, leaders of the scheme in Kent have turned their attention to the 'impact' issue. Teachers participating in the scheme have documented their development work in their portfolios and have analysed it in their critical narrative writing. Here we have readily available rich sources of evidence, containing not only the facts of a particular sequence of events, but a unique account also of how teachers felt about them as they unfolded, with a considerable amount of triangulated evidence about impact on their own professional practice and learning, on pupil learning and on the school as an organization. However, it is important that we try to be clear about what we mean by 'impact' and what we understand by 'learning'.

Defining Learning

There is no shortage of definitions. Nixon et al. (1996) provide a very broad definition, when they describe 'layers of learning'.

> Learning proceeds through different layers: of developing understanding of discrete events or pieces of knowledge to becoming aware of ourselves as persons and then, more significantly, our growing capacity to shape ourselves and, with others, the world around us.
>
> (Nixon et al., 1996: 48)

What Nixon and his colleagues propose here is a vision of 'lifelong learning' in which individuals gradually gain in understanding and the capacity for personal agency. We favour this kind of definition, because we believe that it implies a model of learning that applies equally well to children in school and to their teachers.

Clearly, learning outcomes are also subject to redefinition according to the prevailing notion of what education is for, and, for the purposes of this argument, we need to clarify our understanding of 'learning outcomes'. An 'outcome', we might suggest, is any change in attitude, knowledge, understanding or skill that we can attribute, however indirectly, to some form of deliberate action on behalf of the teacher. In Nixon's terms, this would be an example of 'learning as child-centred development'. However, at the end of the twentieth century in the United Kingdom at least, the prevailing political emphasis appears to be on learning as 'skilling' and 'credentialling' (Parsons, 1999), and learning as 'vocational preparation' and 'selective differentiation' (Nixon, 1996). This will inevitably mean that the most highly prized learning outcomes will relate to achievement as measured in tests and examinations. For example, the Government White Paper 'Excellence for All' (DfEE, 1997b), defines education in idealistic terms as 'the key to creating a society which is dynamic and productive, offering opportunity and fairness for everyone'. The White Paper goes on to state that the means to this end is through the gaining of qualifications:

> The problem with our education system has been that excellence at the top is not matched by high standards for all children. Too many pupils still fail to achieve what they can. Too many leave school with few or no qualifications.
>
> (DfEE, 1997b)

If we used this definition of the 'problem' of education to ascertain the impact of teacher-led inquiry on learning, we would have to establish that the examination results of children whose teachers are participants in the RAP scheme improve.

Is this possible or even desirable, however? We would argue that the attainment of a particular exam score or grade is one of many possible outcomes of learning. We would prefer to think of learning outcomes more broadly in terms of the processes by which children come to understand, know and be able to do things. A learning outcome may be an improvement in attitude or motivation; it could be the ability to complete a particular task or solve a particular problem unaided; it may manifest itself in enhanced self-esteem, improved attendance or prompt completion of homework, and there may be no discernible impact on test or examination scores. Does that render the improvement in learning worthless? Fielding expresses concerns about the 'myopia' of this concentration on examination scores at the expense of a broader conception of education, which is 'informed by democratic values, dispositions and processes that have at their heart a sense of personhood and human flourishing' (1997: 158). However, it is much easier to measure a school's GCSE results than it is to assess its 'democratic values'. White (1997) makes a distinction between an educational 'outcome', such as a school's GCSE scores, and an educational 'goal', which might be to do with something like 'democratic citizenship'. The distinction is perhaps similar to the one Stenhouse (1975) draws, between a *process* model of learning and an *objectives* one. While the latter assumes that knowledge is fixed and value-free, the former renders knowledge problematical and open to reflection and debate.

However, it is by no means 'a truth universally acknowledged' that reflective practice of the kind envisaged by Stenhouse is desirable. Chris Woodhead, HM Chief Inspector of Schools, in his 1999 Annual Lecture, argues that there is no need for teachers to engage in knowledge creation; we already know as much as we need to know; the challenge is to transmit this efficiently and effectively to students in schools, for teaching, he insists, is a craft based on knowledge of what '*must* be taught', of 'the structure that *must* be followed' and of 'classroom competencies'. He sees Stenhouse's 'romanticism' about teachers' professionalism as a 'distraction' from the national agenda of raising standards. However, while he believes that teachers have no right to question the curriculum and assessment policies of a democratically elected government, Woodhead invites them to share his scepticism about educational research, arguing that good teachers have no need of theories of learning. This insistence on teaching as a craft rather than a discipline (note the repetition of 'must' above) and the mistrust of theoretical perspectives, even important and internationally recognized ones such as Howard Gardner's work on 'multiple intelligences' suggests a bleak, gradgrindian view of the educational process.

Reed and Learmonth (1999) believe, on the other hand, that reflective practice is an essential aspect of teachers' professionalism. In particular, they argue that teachers need to be able to recognize, gather, interpret and act on evidence about 'standards in the classroom' if student attainment is to rise. The authors make a useful distinction between 'shallow' and 'deep' approaches to school improvement. Shallow initiatives tend to be short-term and 'related to performance outcomes', while deep school improvement is more long term in scope, is concerned with complex issues, eschews quick and easy answers and relies upon teachers themselves learning how to carry out research into their own practice in order to assess the impact of the strategies they employ. However, it is not sufficient simply to reflect on these matters. What is important is that the teacher has the skills and support to act on these understandings. The time is right, they argue, for school improvement initiatives to focus on classroom processes so that teachers can begin to develop a 'language' with which to account for the impact of what they do on student learning.

Howard Gardner's work on 'multiple intelligences' is helpful in that it opens up the way we might look at learning outcomes. He defines an intelligence as the ability both to solve real problems and difficulties and to create or find problems (Gardner, 1993: 60). This theoretical perspective posits seven types of intelligence that do not develop uniformly in each person and which are given differing emphases within different cultures around the world. Gardner's intelligences are:

1 Linguistic Intelligence
2 Musical Intelligence
3 Logical–Mathematical Intelligence

4   Spatial Intelligence
5   Bodily-Kinaesthetic Intelligence
6   Inter-personal Intelligence
7   Intra-personal Intelligence

(Gardner, 1993)

Barber (1996), unlike Woodhead (1999), believes that the ramifications of Gardner's work are so important for education that not only should all teachers be aware of and make use of his theories in the classroom, but that account should be taken of his ideas when new curricula are being designed. Gipps (1994) adds that we need a curriculum and assessment model that promotes learning 'in many domains'. She regrets the fact that current assessment procedures in the UK education system are still premised on a model of learning that suggests that learning proceeds in a linear and sequential manner and that skills can be broken down into component parts and tested. This leads to teachers in schools 'teaching to the tests' in order to ensure that their students perform well, and, in an era of increased teacher accountability, to prevent questions being asked about their own competence.

Current cognitive theory holds that learning is a process of knowledge construction, and that it is both knowledge-dependent and context-dependent. Nisbet and Shucksmith (1986) argue that a key aspect of learning is *metacognition* which includes the notion of study skills, but goes beyond that to embrace the ability to select and apply appropriate skills to advance learning. The work of Kolb (1984) on learning styles echoes this concern. He posits four types of learner: reflectors, theorists, pragmatists and activists. Most of us have a preference towards one of these learning styles, though with coaching we can improve our ability to manipulate data in all four areas. Nixon et al. (1996), as we have already seen, go further and write of 'layers of learning' in which we come to understand and shape ourselves and the world around us, with the key purpose of learning lying 'through its forming of our powers and capacities, in our unfolding agency' (1996: 49). However, Fullan notes that for students to have this view of learning, their teachers must themselves be lifelong learners, committed to dialogue and collaboration and having the flexibility to manage continuous change; in short, they must possess the skills of the change agent, skills that Fullan argues 'each and every educator' (1993: 13) should strive to attain. He suggests that the effective change agent has four core capacities: personal vision-building, inquiry, mastery and collaboration (illustrated in the case studies in Chapters 7–8). These cannot be practised in isolation, but have to be honed in the context of an institution which encourages them. We would argue that the school-based nature of the RAP model provides a framework within which the individual can develop these capacities. Teachers' professional learning is, therefore, intimately bound up with, and at least as important as student learning, and teacher learning can only take place within the context of the organization.

This is a view which also makes a good fit with criteria the TTA established in 1998 as a basis for the funding of CPD programmes. The documentation issued by the TTA in 1998 said that, in order to receive funding, a programme must:

> have as its main objective, the improvement of pupils' performance through the improvement of school teachers' and headteachers' professional knowledge, understanding and skills and their effectiveness in teaching and/or leadership and management.

(TTA, 1998)

If we are to assess the impact of participants' development work then it would seem to make sense to try to establish the degree to which the RAP model facilitates improvements in teachers' learning, institutional development and student outcomes.

Researching Impact

Reflective action planning shares with many other CPD programmes and school improvement projects, the aim of bringing about improvements in instructional practice and, consequently raised pupil attainment. However, what we believe is unique about RAP is its explicitness about the strategies teachers should adopt in order to maximize impact. The model described in Chapter 4 embodies both a series of steps and a conceptual framework by which we can better understand the relationship between the teacher, the organization and the learner. We argue that the RAP model does not simply offer a recipe for teacher research; rather, it provides a structure within which individuals can carry out a strategic, planned and integrated programme of action. Underlying the model is an assumption that the impact of a teacher's work is likely to be greater when they have engaged in personal vision building and personal development planning, consulted and collaborated with other professionals and taken steps to change practice and evaluate outcomes.

Following on from the work of the ESACS project (see Chapter 5), we have begun to examine more closely the impact of teacher-led development work by focusing on the evidence compiled in the participants' portfolios generated within the reflective action planning framework. This material is a particularly rich source of data as, unlike other documentary evidence that we might find in schools such as policy documents or minutes of meetings, portfolios and dissertations are deliberately reflective documents, and so will tend to explore incidents in an analytical way rather than merely report them. Institutional documents are normally couched in specialized language, are intended for specific audiences and contribute to an ongoing narrative about the decision-making processes, key events and developments of the organization (Atkinson and Coffey, 1997). However, the writing of participants in the

RAP groups, while still adhering to a set of codes and conventions derived from the academic requirements of the HEI, is distinguished by its variety of registers. A typical portfolio will a contain biographical account in which the participant reflects on her own professional history and educational values. There will also be accounts of professional action taken, with supporting evidence taken from interviews, direct observation or other forms of inquiry; in addition, the participant will reflect critically on the meanings of these events, perhaps referring to research and school improvement literature. In addition, there may well be documents written for other professional audiences in the school which aim to stimulate debate, initiate change or simply report on the participant's development work. Finally, because of the sequence of activities implied by the reflective action model and the assessment criteria that participants' work is judged against, participants' accounts tend to be structured in similar ways, making comparisons between a number of folders much easier.

We have recently analysed a selection of the very large number of portfolios and dissertations that have now been produced using the RAP framework. This analysis has proved to be a very rich research activity in itself that provides ample and convincing evidence that teachers have indeed been able to bring about positive changes in their own practice, make significant contributions to institutional development and have an impact on children's learning. It is clear that the way in which participants are asked to structure their development work itself appears to maximize the potential for impact.

What follows is an exploration of how evidence of impact can be found within the participants' own submissions. We present brief summaries of the work of just three teachers and highlight the way their own compilations of evidence and narrative accounts can be trawled for evidence of impact. We have chosen Elise's story because it tells us a lot about personal learning, Gloria's because it tells us a lot about institutional learning, and Gillian's because it tells us about the processes of student learning. In each case we use the sub-headings 'Personal-Vision Building', 'Consultation and Collaboration' and 'Changing Practice', corresponding to some of the key elements of the model set out in Chapter 3 and described in detail in Chapter 4.

Elise's Story: Impact on Teachers' Professional Learning

Personal Vision-Building

Elise, when she began her most recent cycle of development work, had just been promoted to the position of Special Needs Co-ordinator (SENCO) at St. James' School. She had high expectations of herself, and the problem she identified at the start of her development work was how best to undertake this complex, many-faceted new role. She recalled some of her own experiences of educational failure while at school, describing the sense of shame, anger and humiliation she felt at not being able to complete a woodwork project – a fluorescent fish. She saw her main responsibility as one of helping to prevent children at St James' experiencing that same sense of failure:

> and that for me will be the challenge – spotting the children who need help to create the basic shape of an idea in their mind. Once they have that, then maybe they'll be able to paint the pattern on their own.
>
> (Marlow, 1999: 13)

The conflict she identified early on was between her own previous teaching experiences in largely mixed ability environments and the situation she inherited of a small withdrawal group to whom she was to teach English, maths and science. Somekh (1993) argues that our values are not always clear to us because they are so deeply woven into our everyday routines and practices. For Elise, this painstaking and detailed clarification of values was an essential step in planning her future action. It would have been easy for her to concentrate on the administrative and managerial aspects of her role, but her reflections on her own schooldays helped her to focus primarily on promoting success in learning as the key facet of her role.

Consultation and Collaboration

Elise entered enthusiastically into her new role with a desire to listen to both colleagues and children. Her case study records in detail the changing perceptions of her target group of Year Eight students over a period of one academic year. It is clear from her account that the students' voices were a crucial support to her in planning teaching and learning strategies. She was particularly struck by the sense of failure that they brought with them at the start of the year: 'The impact pupil perception of success has on motivation and behaviour was fascinating to observe and distressing in its implications' (Marlow, 1999: 85).

Elise's understanding of the ways she could best help these students was formed as much by listening to their own accounts, carefully studying their written responses and observing their performance in class as by any 'expert' help she sought in specialist literature. For example, she devotes considerable time in her case study to tracking one of her pupils, Damien, as he wrote a story over the space of one week. She notes in exhaustive detail the changes he made to the various drafts of his narrative, the help he needed and his own comments and behaviour during the process. Elise has in effect compiled a case record that shows her planning, refining and evaluating as she teaches, in the manner of Schon's (1983) reflective practitioner. Elise's way of working highlights the importance we need to attach to the processes of learning as well as to its outcomes. Thus, another key feature of the RAP scheme is the emphasis it places on participants attempting to reach their own self-generated understandings of situations rather than relying on received wisdom. Elliott puts it succinctly: 'Improving practice involves jointly considering the quality of both outcomes and processes' (Elliott, 1991: 50).

Collaboration does not always have positive outcomes. Elise's professional learning was further enhanced by the attempts she made to collaborate with colleagues over the way students with special educational needs could best be supported throughout the school. In a series of meetings she set up with teachers, she was disconcerted by their apparent lack of will to take responsibility for students' learning, preferring to discuss disciplinary routines or argue for difficult pupils to be removed from the school altogether. On reflection, she believes the sequence of meetings she arranged to have been examples of what Andy Hargreaves (1996) calls 'contrived collegiality'. This experience inspired her to try to address the problem of fostering genuine collaboration between teachers as her next round of development work. We see that, by reflecting on professional disappointment, Elise was able to move through the frustration and pain of not meeting her aims to a more clear-headed appraisal of what was wrong and how she could address it in future.

Changing Practice

Elise's critical narrative charts in considerable detail how her 'withdrawal group' responded to the various activities she carried out with them. Her own understanding of how children learn or are prevented from learning was clearly enhanced by the care with which she selected and analysed examples of students' work and reflected on the effectiveness of the strategies she had employed. In a section of her case study devoted to the use of writing frames, she writes:

> I was left with two fundamental questions: was the frame itself a constraint, militating against pupils being able to develop ideas more fully? And had the lack of opportunity to discuss and plan ideas verbally restricted their ability to write a more developed response to the task?
>
> (Marlow, 1999: 98)

Woodhead (1999) declares that teacher reflection has nothing to offer the profession. It is difficult to support such a notion when we see practitioners analysing with such care and attention to detail the effects of their interventions on pupil learning.

Elise highlights near the end of her narrative the effect this process of 'trial and error' has had on her professional learning: 'Reviewing my letter of application for the post of head of Learning Support illuminated for me how much my professional thinking has developed this year' (Marlow, 1999: 135). It is clear that the process of reflective action planning has had a significant impact on how Elise sees her role and professional identity. She goes on to give a powerful list of teaching and learning strategies she now believes 'work', the most important one of which is:

> providing pupils with the chance to talk to a listening adult who can advise and guide their progress in the context of an understanding of the other factors that affect the pupils' ability to concentrate and learn in school.
>
> (Marlow, 1999: 136)

We see in this account a teacher who, in reviewing the year's development work, has re-defined her role from that of an expert who delivers technical support to children with learning difficulties to that of a counsellor-educator who engages with students not solely on an intellectual level, but an emotional and affective one too.

One of the most dramatic moments for the reader in Elise's writing comes near the end when she links her work into the wider discourse of the school as a learning organization. She now sees as 'central to my values' a situation where all students see school as an inclusive, enabling institution with recognizable opportunities for success. This realization on the teacher's part that her own values form part of a wider educational debate is a powerful one, and one which we believe the RAP model is instrumental in encouraging.

Gloria's Story: Impact on the Institution

Personal Vision–Building

Gloria, head of a sixth form of around 160 students at St. James' School, perceived a sense of discontinuity between the 'pastoral' and the 'academic' systems concerning post-16 students in the school. It appeared to her that more effective communication was needed if students' needs were to be fully met. Her aim was to put in place systems that would improve what she called 'the learning culture' of the school.

Consultation and Collaboration

Gloria set out to gather further information from four main sources: readings from the literature on post-16 issues, attendance at appropriate teachers' courses, becoming a member of the school's curriculum working party and interviewing representative groups of students. This deliberative and planned approach to information gathering is a feature of the scheme which enables participants to 'triangulate' their perceptions of a situation more effectively. She put together a report based on the information she had gathered to be presented to the whole staff during a development day. Her critical narrative indicated an awareness of the scope of her work: 'I felt that through my inquiry and action, my aims were becoming clearer, and that I was working with the whole school rather than in isolation' (Rylatt, 1997: 15).

Changing Practice

Gloria's chosen solution to the problem was to set up a regular programme of personal tutorials for all post-16 students in the school. She was aware that such a system, not having hitherto operated, might meet with resistance from colleagues who would question the extra workload implied. In order to address this, she set out from the start to involve her ten form tutors in the process of planning the scheme, to give them a sense of 'ownership and involvement' in the scheme in which they would play 'a pivotal and active role' (Rylatt 1997: 18). This highlights the importance of collaboration as a feature of the scheme. Gloria's inquiry was motivated by a strong personal vision of the kind of learning community she wanted sixth form students to be part of. However, she knew that the only way she would be able to see that vision through was by working with others, sharing it with them, but allowing them to shape, modify and build on it, so that it became a genuinely shared, collectively owned vision.

Gloria displayed, in the setting up of this project, the ability to work with three key groups in the school: students, colleagues and senior managers to ensure that there was a shared understanding of what the tutorial system was designed to achieve. It could be argued that she displayed 'mastery', which Fullan (1993) argues involves a keen awareness of the processes by which personal and institutional change takes place. Gloria herself acknowledges the role the RAP model may have played in this: 'I have thoroughly enjoyed the dialogue which this work has prompted me to initiate on a number of levels with students, tutors, senior teachers in my school and teachers in other establishments' (Rylatt, 1997). Here, Gloria is celebrating in a modest way the realization that her work has enabled her to make a significant contribution to the development of professional discourse within the school.

As she came to the end of this cycle of development, Gloria wrote that she felt herself to be growing in confidence as a change agent and expressed satisfaction that 'the impact of my work is important to the school as well as the sixth form' (Rylatt, 1997: 30). This appears to support Fullan's (1993: 15) view that 'personal purpose is the route to organizational change'. Gloria's narrative ends with the assertion that the results of this inquiry have inspired her to begin another phase of development work and writes that the development work she has carried out with students and teachers has deepened her interest in 'dialogue and democracy' in schools. She now sees the tutorial system not merely as a technical solution to the problem of student target setting, but potentially as a crucial element in a learning community in which the nurturing of the student voice is seen as a fundamental duty. This has important links with Elise's experience described above. Both Elise and Gloria began with an essentially technical 'problem' to solve. However, as they explored the issues in more detail, read more widely and worked more closely with others, they began to see that what they were in fact working on was the alignment of strongly held personal beliefs and values with practice.

Gillian's Story: Impact on Student Learning

Personal Vision-Building

Gillian, a modern languages teacher, was concerned that the Year 11 students she taught appeared to be underachieving in their German lessons. She decided that the main problem seemed to be a lack of motivation and engagement. In order to tackle this she had previously devised an ambitious set of self-help materials that students could use at home to support their learning of German. However, she quickly realized that the class resented rather than welcomed her efforts, seeing it as extra work rather than learning support. She set herself the challenge of working with this class in order to find out why they were so disengaged, and to increase their motivation and success in German.

The importance of the 'clarification of values' phase of the RAP process is to encourage participants to select with some precision specific areas of practice to focus on. It should follow that the sharper the focus, the more successful the impact on pupil learning will be.

Consultation and Collaboration

When Gillian circulated a questionnaire to help her understand why the students seemed to lack engagement, she found the responses quite upsetting: the students were unhappy about her intervention in their learning, even though she perceived herself to be working hard on their behalf. After she had recovered from the shock of realizing that they saw her efforts in this way, Gillian began to reflect on the real meaning of these comments (Tripp, 1984). She came to the conclusion that her pupils did not appreciate that learning might depend not only on what she as teacher did, but also on what they as students would need to do. The questionnaire results revealed a resistance in particular to learning vocabulary out of class. Gillian felt that they were expressing resistance to taking responsibility for their learning. The importance of this incident is to highlight the fact that while 'listening to the student's voice' rightly implies respect for and active seeking out of pupils' views, it does not always mean that what they say will be palatable to the teacher or even that she should agree with those views. The teacher has the analytical tools to interpret what children say, and devise action on the basis of it. We would argue that the process of evidence gathering itself has an impact on children's learning, as interviews and questionnaires, when designed with care, require the students to reflect on their own learning preferences and process, thus developing their metacognitive processes.

Changing Practice

She felt confident that this 'reconnaisance' phase (Elliott, 1991) enabled her to design lesson activities much more closely geared to the needs of her pupils. Gillian's conclusion after her evidence-gathering phase was that her initial attempt to support her students' independent learning had failed to take account of their perceptions of themselves as learners:

> My priorities were not necessarily theirs. I realized that in order to teach them how to be good language learners I would have to create an atmosphere in which they would want to be good language learners.
>
> (Extract from portfolio)

Gillian's main support came from her head of department. The chances of inquiry having a successful impact increase when there is dialogue with line managers who can offer crucial support in directing time and resources to support the teacher undertaking development work. However, Gillian decided to go beyond the boundaries of her subject, and spent some time talking to colleagues who taught the same class and even observed the same group of students in other lessons so that she could get a more rounded view of their whole educational diet and see for herself how they behaved in other lessons. The requirement to negotiate and collaborate can be seen to also have a positive impact on student learning, therefore, as in Gillian's case we see her both actively recruiting support for her work and enlarging her understanding of the needs of her students.

Gillian eventually arrived at the idea of introducing her students to a metalanguage with which to evaluate, in German, the learning activities Gillian set them. The idea had come from one of her students who had written in the original questionnaire that the class did not have the opportunity to speak what she called 'everyday German'. Gillian saw this request as an ideal opportunity to introduce to her students the idea that both she and they were responsible for the effectiveness of lessons, while at the same time working on their understanding of the target language:

> It seemed to me, in emancipatory terms, that this was a very important speech act, as so often pupils are unable to comment on what is going on in the language class or to express satisfaction or dissatisfaction in the target language, as they do not have access to the language needed to do this. Yet griping about the lessons is probably one of the most frequent speech acts encountered in schools.
>
> (Extract from portfolio)

Gillian found that the atmosphere in her classroom improved dramatically. The same students who had appeared so reluctant to take responsibility responded positively to Gillian's attempts to give them language they felt they had a need to use, as opposed to only the language specified by the course book. The message for Gillian seemed to be that students take responsibility for their learning when they are given responsibility.

Gillian's final reflections on the two terms' development work she had carried out show the extent to which she had reconceptualized the role played by students and teacher in the classroom. Like Elise, her original concern had been a technical one, but by the end of the cycle of inquiry Gillian saw the classroom in much more sophisticated terms, describing the language learning classroom as 'a rehearsal for a theatrical production' with the teacher as director, using the curriculum materials as a form of script which has to be brought to life and modified where necessary by the actors or pupils. This is a powerful metaphor that suggests a model of learning that is creative, flexible and dynamic.

Conclusion

When formulating the focus for their development work, it can be seen that the teachers tend not to articulate their intentions so much in terms of educational outcomes, but rather in terms of processes; it is the quality of classroom or organizational performance on which they concentrate. RAP group leaders may well decide that they need to challenge participants on the way they think about outcomes, but, at this stage in our research and in this particular context, it makes sense to study 'impact' primarily in terms of the impact on the processes of individual or organizational learning. This has shown that there is persuasive and consistent evidence that the RAP model provides a framework within which individuals' development work can be seen to bring about improvements in participants' professional learning, organizational learning and student learning.

We need to recognize that schools as organizations are complex and problematical and are continually changing and developing through the interplay of various internal and external factors. In compartmentalizing the issues and fragmenting the problems, we lose the 'big picture'. In order to understand the complexity of the process of school improvement, a holistic, organic approach is needed (Fink, 1998; Senge, 1990). The relationships between characteristics of school effectiveness, conditions for school improvement, teaching and learning are not linear and mechanistic; we have to look beyond the lists of criteria and competencies and delve beneath the statistics and performance tables in order to develop understanding through continued inquiry, exploration and dialogue.

It is the school's intelligent application of knowledge about schools, improvement, learning and teaching which strengthens its capacity to raise standards and enhance students' progress and achievement (MacGilchrist et al., 1997). This does not happen simply through the implementation of multiple initiatives resulting in superficial changes of behaviour (Fullan, 1991), but is encouraged through fostering a culture within the school in which everyone recognizes the importance of, and takes responsibility for, their own and others' learning. Senge's language captures the creativity, passion and moral purpose of such a 'learning organization': 'where people can continually expand their capacity to create the results they truly desire, where new and expansive patterns of thinking are nurtured, where collective aspiration is set free ...' (Senge, 1990:3).

We believe that the RAP approach to school improvement empowers teachers to reach a greater understanding, individually and collectively, of the many interdependent factors influencing educational experience and learning outcomes, which leads them to develop their own and others' practice accordingly and to effect appropriate change. It is unrealistic to try to isolate RAP from other factors and processes interacting towards improvement in school and classroom. It is futile to try to attribute measurable increases in children's attainment to their teachers' participation in the RAP process within one school or across the whole programme, although quantitative analysis might well be part of an individual teacher's inquiry process. Instead we have offered, through case study, authentic glimpses of the RAP process in action, thereby making visible its impact on personal, institutional and student learning.

Conclusion

Teachers and the Creation of Professional Knowledge

We have articulated and illustrated a model of school improvement which enables teachers to make more of a difference in their schools by making a greater contribution to development work which will result in improved learning outcomes for their students.

We see this publication as part of a more widespread focus on the resurgence of teacher professionalism reflected in the creation of a General Teaching Council. In 'The Learning Game', Michael Barber, the current chair of the government's Standards and Effectiveness Unit, highlights the need for teachers to 'reassert their professional judgement' (Barber, 1996: 197). He argues that the key to rebuilding teachers' self-confidence lies in a concept of professional development that is founded not on narrowly conceived ideas about INSET, but on the idea of the teacher as a lifelong learner who is a member of a learning, research-based profession: 'Teachers should not have the power to determine education policy: nor should they be slaves to it. Success depends on them making sense of it for themselves' (Barber, 1996: 197).

We believe that the approach to school improvement described here provides a structure or framework within which teachers, working with the culture and values of their schools, can do much more than 'make sense of' policy; they can exercise leadership, manage change and contribute to the wide professional discourse which helps to shape policy at both local and national levels.

We hope that we have demonstrated that schemes using this approach to enhance teachers' agency can have real impact, not only on the professional learning of teachers as individuals, but also on the capacity of their organizations to manage change. It is abundantly clear from our experience and from the evidence gathered in the course of our research that such effects have a consequent impact on pupils' learning. The fact that both CANTIS and CANTARNET continue to flourish and that teachers maintain links with the network long after they have completed their master's degrees suggests that the participating schools and teachers are convinced of the benefits. It is also encouraging to note that the RAP model has been taken up and adapted for use in other contexts and partnerships which include LEAs. In the HESCAM project (1998–9), for example, the Hertfordshire LEA entered into partnership with the University of Cambridge and six secondary schools to support school improvement to be led by two teachers from each school (Frost et al., 1999).

Partnership is the Key

We have emphasized throughout that partnership is the key to success: partnership between teachers and their colleagues in school, partnership between HEIs and schools, and partnerships involving LEAs. However, the pursuit of genuine and productive partnerships constitutes a major challenge for all concerned. There is a need for robust negotiations leading to agreements in which there is clarity about complementary roles and responsibilities. The schools need to ensure not only that they support and facilitate the process, but also that they embrace the consequences of nurturing such an engine for change in their midst. Enhanced critical discourse within a school can lead to turbulence which, if handled positively, can be creative and productive. HEIs, on the other hand, also have to be prepared to adapt in order to be able to play their part. This may mean reviewing structures of accreditation or rethinking what counts as academic work. Dominant ways of conceptualizing research may constitute an obstacle to the sort of partnership described here, and some university lecturers' views of their roles as teacher educators and consultants may need to be re-examined.

There is clearly a moral dimension to partnership, and we need to guard against the development of relationships which might be exploitative or unequal. For example, it has been suggested that, in their relationships with schools, HEIs have engaged in 'academic imperialism'. Positivistic forms of research have been seen by some as exploitative in that outsiders gather data from schools in order to publish esoteric papers in academic journals without giving anything back to the teachers or their schools. Action research has tended to be portrayed as an antidote to this, but despite the emancipatory rhetoric there are suggestions that the university departments of education (UDEs) have continued to be imperialistic. Elliott, although a leading advocate of action research, questioned this:

> Action research and the 'teachers as researchers' movement are enthusiastically promoted in academia. But the question is: are the academics transforming the methodology of teacher-based educational inquiry into a form which enables them to manipulate and control teachers' thinking in order to reproduce the central assumptions which have underpinned a contemplative academic culture detached from the practices of everyday life?
>
> (Elliott, 1991: 14)

We have argued here that the reflective action planning approach largely avoids this problem, but, in so doing, it might be said that the universities have been colonized by the school teaching community in such a way that their traditional mission is being seriously undermined. It has been argued (Nixon, 1996) that the universities are becoming depoliticized institutions serving social labour which neutralizes their traditional role in the democratic process.

Impact on the Role of the Academic Worker

Towards the latter stages of the ESACS project research (see Chapter 5), we investigated the impact of our innovatory work on the role of the academic worker. It had been suggested by some colleagues that the working conditions for the HEI tutor had been impoverished in the reflective action planning scenario. It could be argued that successive governments have taken steps to establish a market economy whereby the higher education sector is thrust into a service role; the development of 'partnership' approaches in teacher education and other professional contexts can thus be seen as contributing to the diminution of the traditional role of the universities in society. Overall it could be said that, in the reflective action planning scenario, the HEI tutors' working conditions are problematic to say the least; the role of the visiting academic worker is not an easy one. Some aspects of these conditions may seem relatively trivial, such as the fact that the sessions often take place in rooms which are uncomfortable, inadequately heated or badly equipped, and that the tutor often has to stop on the way to the school to pick up refreshments for the group. Some are seriously time-consuming, such as the fact that the tutor has to travel to the school not only to teach on the programme and provide tutorial support, but also to negotiate and plan with the school co-ordinator. Other aspects affect the tutor's role in a more fundamental way, for example, the fact that the group sessions take place at the end of the school's teaching day means that participants are often tired and distracted by the events of the day, and the requirement to respond to events, emerging priorities and issues within a group session constitutes a considerable challenge to the tutor in terms of their situational understanding and breadth of expertise. There are also challenges which spring from the need to be sensitive to the micro-political tensions within the school and to observe a somewhat fragile etiquette.

It is perhaps not surprising therefore that academics who were asked to work in these sorts of ways tended to have mixed feelings about the approach. One story that HEI tutors might tell is that 'marketization' and the 'discourse of competitiveness' has led to the 'discourse of insecurity' (Edwards, 1997) and that the impoverishment of the tutors' working conditions results in the neutralization of the critical stance that academics might normally be expected to adopt. This can be seen as simply another dimension of the 'decline of donnish dominion' which has been taking place since the Second World War (Halsey, 1992).

Since the transfer of the funding for Continuing Professional Development (CPD) to the Teacher Training Agency (TTA) in England and Wales, UDEs have come under increasing pressure from the state to provide programmes which address more directly national priorities as specified by the TTA. This entails a greater emphasis on partnership arrangements where programmes are jointly planned to respond to particular needs expressed at local and regional levels. Programmes are also more likely to be jointly led and taught by local authority advisory staff and/or experienced teachers. There is to be a greater emphasis on school-focused and school-based programmes linked to the priorities such as 'school improvement' and 'leadership and management'. In order to attract TTA funding, universities will also need to deliver programmes in which teachers, headteachers and those aspiring to senior management are trained according to the TTA's 'standards' or competence specifications.

These sorts of developments are already having an impact on the nature of lecturers' work in that they demand a great deal more from lecturers in terms of time and ingenuity. For example, partnership arrangements require careful negotiation and joint planning. School-based schemes require a great deal of flexibility and a willingness to adapt to changing circumstances. They require lecturers to be able to respond to the particular needs of clients and to cope with the inconvenience of travel to remote school sites. Accreditation arrangements require the preparation of a great deal of guidance material to support teachers in independent reflection and inquiry. So the day-to-day work of academics is affected quite dramatically, partly in terms of the nature of the tasks that have to be undertaken, and partly in terms of the volume of time consumed.

However, the impact of the TTA initiative goes beyond affecting the nature of UDEs' work with schools; it also entails and even demands a review of institutional systems for decision making, planning and quality assurance. A growth in the off-site, partnership-based sort of work described above means that it becomes more difficult to ensure comparability of standards which creates the need for more detailed criteria and procedural guidelines as well as more effective systems for scrutinizing new programmes and assuring their quality.

Our own dilemma stems from our intense involvement over a period of five to six years in research and development work, which could be said to have helped to usher in such partnership and school-based work. Of course, it is not true that the nature of our work is wholly determined by the state or by the market place; our own account would stress the central role of our professional values. However, our dilemma pivots on our growing awareness of the tension between these determinants and the extent to which the rhetoric of teacher empowerment may have acted as a smokescreen for the dismantling of the professionalism of university teachers (Fielding, 1996).

The picture is further complicated by the fact that the innovation described in this book has largely been taken forward by a new breed of academic workers referred to earlier as 'associate tutors', most of whom have their roots in schools with only a toe-hold in the university (see Chapter 3). They have embraced the role both competently and enthusiastically. The idea of the associate tutor was established from the beginning because it was considered essential that the two collaborators should inhabit each other's domains in order to develop a shared perspective. Thus, the HEI lecturer would teach some lessons in the school every week and the teacher collaborator would attend examination board meetings at the HEI, for example. The fact that both the HEI tutor and the teacher collaborator were engaged in scholastic activity was seen to be essential to the maintenance of an appropriate level of discourse and an engagement with the literature on educational research and school improvement.

In discussions with associate tutors involved in the CANTIS scheme, Jon Nixon's thesis (1996) about the depoliticization of the university and the proletarianization of academics was largely rejected. Their scepticism was not because they thought it was untrue about what is happening to universities in general, but because they see themselves not as members of a self-governing academic community free to criticize social policy and the like, but rather as members of an associated community which includes both teachers and academic workers who share a commitment to a common endeavour. It was agreed that what is important is that the values of higher education need to be nurtured and explicitly pursued, not just in the university cloisters but in professional contexts such as schools, teacher networks and any other site of intellectual and moral endeavour. This viewpoint requires that the boundaries of both the universities and the schools should be more permeable to allow a deeper level of interaction and partnership.

Knowledge Creation

After all, schools and HEIs share a common enterprise in that they are both in the business of knowledge generation. Hargreaves has argued (see also Chapter 8) that the educational research system in Britain needs to be reformed because it has such little impact on educational practice; he suggests that teachers need to be involved in 'tinkering' with educational ideas and practices in order to 'transfer' them from one context to another and to 'transpose' them through a process of exploration and adaptation (Hargreaves, 1998). This way of thinking accommodates both the 'vision' inherent in national policy priorities and the 'voice' of teachers for whom it has to make sense. The HEIs have a vital part to play in working with teachers and schools, firstly to make their own publicly funded research intelligible to teachers and relevant to practice, and secondly to act as brokers, facilitating teachers in their knowledge creation and networking. We put forward the reflective action planning model as a vehicle for enabling teachers and academics to collaborate in the production, adaptation and dissemination of professional knowledge.

Using this model, teachers are collecting and presenting evidence of their development work in the form of portfolios which contain 'case records' (Stenhouse, 1978). They are invited to disseminate their work not only to their colleagues in school, but also through contact with other groups in the network and at the regular network conferences. As they gather experience, they go on to produce case studies in the form of dissertations and shorter articles for *The Enquirer*, which is published simultaneously on the World Wide Web and in the traditional paper format; they are thus able to contribute to the generation of public knowledge about education. These accounts together with the 'contacts list' also published on the Internet enable other teachers to access this rich store of knowledge and expertise, and it is particularly satisfying that the use of the Internet means that the whole archive is always available and can now be downloaded by anyone with a computer terminal and rudimentary knowledge about its use. There is enormous potential here for professional researchers in the UDEs to engage in the synthesis and meta-analysis of this material to ensure that the knowledge generated is systematized and made coherent. In this way, we can develop further the collaboration between schools and universities.

Having developed and worked with this model over a long period of time, it is our experience that it is realistic to aspire to equitable partnerships in which all those involved share a commitment to evidence-based discourse aimed at the improvement of the quality of learning. We have been privileged to work within a professional community in which school teachers, university academics and those occupying a zone between the two domains have been able to engage in inquiry-based strategic action to improve their practice as teachers, managers, consultants and researchers, and to change the structures which shape it. The combination of these different perspectives fosters a climate which is characterized by challenge and rigour as well as support and encouragement. In such a climate, professional knowledge can be renewed and generated; collective understanding can be developed, and individuals can make meaning of the complexities of educational processes.

References

Abbott, R. et al. (1988) *GRIDS School Handbooks*, Harrow: Longmans.

Ainscow, M., Hopkins, D., Southworth, G. and West, M. (1994) *Creating the Conditions for School Improvement*, London: David Fulton.

Angus, L. (1993) '"New" Leadership and the Possibility of Educational Reform', in J. Smyth (ed.), *A Socially Critical View of the Self-managing School*, London: Falmer Press.

Argyris, C. and Schon, D. (1996) *Organizational Learning II*, Reading, MA: Addison-Wesley.

Atkinson, P. and Coffey, A. (1997) 'Analysing Documentary Realities', in D. Silverman (ed.), *Qualitative Research: Theory, Method and Practice*, London: Sage.

Ball, S.J. (1987) *The Micro-Politics of the School: Towards a Theory of School Organization*, London: Methuen.

—— (1990) 'Management as Moral Technology', in S.J. Ball (ed.), *Foucault and Education: Discipline and Knowledge*, London: Routledge, 153–66.

—— (1999) 'Labour, Learning and the Economy: A "Policy Sociology" Perspective', *Cambridge Journal of Education* 29(2): 195–206.

Bangs, J. (1998) 'Yes, but…', *Improving Schools* 1(1): 20–1.

Barber, M. (1996) *The Learning Game: Arguments for an Education Revolution*, London: Gollancz.

—— (1999) 'Seven Pillars to Support a Top Class 21st Century System', *Times Educational Supplement*, 6 February, 20.

Barnard, N. (1999) 'Teacher Panel to Block "Irrelevant" Research', *Times Educational Supplement*, 17 September, 14.

Barnett, R. (1990) *The Idea of Higher Education*, Buckingham: SRHE/Open University Press.

Bassey, M. (1995) *Creating Education Through Research*, Newark: Kirklington Press.

Bell, G. (1989) 'Action Inquiry Networks', in P. Ovens and A. Edwards (eds), *CARN Bulletin 9B: Partnership in Teacher Research*, Norwich: CARN Publications, University of East Anglia, 56–64.

Bennis, W., Benne, K. and Chin, R. (1969) *The Planning of Change*, New York: Holt, Rinehart and Winston.

Bernstein, B. (1970) 'Education Cannot Compensate for Society', *New Society* 387, 344–7.

Bridges, D. (1996) 'Teacher Education: The Poverty of Pragmatism', in R. McBride (ed.), *Teacher Education Policy: Some Issues Arising from Research and Practice*, London: Falmer Press, 247–56.

Bridges, D. and Husbands, C. (1996) *Consorting and Collaborating in the Education Market Place*, London: Falmer Press.

Budge, D. (1999) 'Research Focus: "Medicine men have the cure"', *Times Educational Supplement*, 10 September, 26.

Burgess, R. (1985) 'In the Company of teachers: Key Informants and the Study of a Comprehensive School', in R. Burgess (ed.), *Strategies of Educational Research: Qualitative Methods*, Lewes: Falmer Press, 79–100.

CACE (Central Advisory Council for Education) (1967) *Children and Their Primary Schools* (Plowden Report), London: HMSO.

CANTARNET ://www.cant.ac.uk/depts/acad/teached/cantarnet/cantarnet.htm

Carr, W. and Kemmis, S. (1986) *Becoming Critical: Education, Knowledge and Action Research*, Lewes: Falmer Press.

Castells, M. (1996) *The Information Age: Economy, Society and Culture*, Vol. 1, *The Rise of the Network Society*, Oxford: Blackwell.

Chang-Wells, G.L. and Wells, G. (1997) 'Modes of Discourse for Living, Learning and Teaching', in S. Hollingsworth (ed.), *International Action Research: A Casebook for Educational Reform*, London: Falmer Press, 147–56.

Cortazzi, M. (1993) *Narrative Analysis*, London: Falmer Press.

Deans, S. (1997) 'Defending Media Education as a School Subject: Reclaiming Curriculum Development Through Action Research', *The Enquirer*, Spring: 1–2.

Department for Education (1992) *Initial Teacher Training (Secondary Phase)* (Circular 9/92), London: DFE.

Department for Education and Employment (DfEE) (1997a) *Connecting the Learning Society: National Grid for Learning, The Government's Consultation Paper*, London: HMSO.

—— (1997b) *Excellence in Schools*, Presented to Parliament by the Secretary of State for Education and Employment by Command of Her Majesty, London: DfEE.

—— (1998) *The Grid: Your Views, Public Response to the Government's Proposals for a National Grid For Learning*, London: HMSO.

Department of Education and Science (DES) (1972) *Teacher Education and Training* (The James Report), London: HMSO.

—— (1989) *Planning for School Development: Advice to Governors, Headteachers and Teachers*, London: HMSO.

Durrant, J. (1998) 'Editorial', *The Enquirer*, Summer: 1–2.

Easen, P. (1985) *Making School-centred INSET Work*, London: Open University/Croom Helm.

Edwards, R. (1997) *Changing Places: Flexibility, Lifelong Learning and a Learning Society*, London: Routledge.

Elliott, J. (1981) *Action Research: A Framework for Self-Evaluation in Schools*, TIQL Working paper No. 1. mimeo, Cambridge: Cambridge Institute of Education.

—— (1991) *Action Research For Educational Change*, Buckingham: Open University Press.

—— (1993a) 'Professional Education and the Idea of a Practical Science', in J. Elliott (ed.), *Restructuring Teacher Education*, London: Falmer, 65–85.

References

—— (1993b) 'What Have We Learned from Action Research in School-based Evaluation?', *Educational Action Research* 1: 175–86.

—— (1996a) 'School Effectiveness Research and Its Critics: Alternative Visions of Schooling', *Cambridge Journal of Education* 26: 199–224.

—— (1996b) 'The Origins and History of CARN', *The Enquirer*, Summer: 1, 13.

—— (1998a) *The Curriculum Experiment: Meeting the Challenge of Social Change*, Buckingham: Open University Press.

—— (1998b) *Living With Ambiguity And Contradiction: The Challenges for Educational Research in Positioning Itself for the 21st Century*, key-note address, European Conference for Educational Research (ECER), Ljubljana.

Elliott, J. and Sarland, C. (1995) 'A Study of "Teachers as Researchers" in the Context of Award-bearing Courses and Research Degrees', *British Educational Research Journal* 21: 371–86.

Enquirer, The (1996–9)://www.cant.ac.uk/depts/acad/teached/cantarnet/cantarnet.htm

Evans, L. (1998) *Teacher Morale, Job Satisfaction and Motivation*, London: Paul Chapman Publishing.

Fidler, B. (1989) 'Staff Appraisal: Theory, Concepts and Experience in Other Organizations and Problems of Adaptation to Education', in C. Riches and C. Morgan (eds), *Human Resource Management in Education*, Buckingham: Open University Press, 190–207.

Fielding, M. (1996) 'Empowerment: Emancipation or Enervation?', *Journal of Education Policy* 11, 399–417.

—— (1997) 'Beyond School Effectiveness and School Improvement: Lighting the Slow Fuse of Possibility', in J. White and M. Barber (eds), *Perspectives on School Effectiveness and School Improvement*, London: Institute of Education, University of London, 137–60.

Fink, D. (1998) 'Confronting Complexity: A Framework for Action', in *Improving Schools* 1(3): 54–8.

Firestone, W. and Pennell, J. (1997) 'Designing State Sponsored Teacher Networks: A Comparison of Two Cases', *American Educational Research Journal* 34: 237–66.

Frost, D. (1993) 'The Role of Higher Education in School-Based Professional Development', unpublished paper presented at the Annual Conference of the British Educational Research Association, University of Liverpool.

—— (1995) 'The ESACS (Evaluating a School-based Award bearing Curriculum Development Scheme) Project: A Code of Practice', *Educational Action Research* 3(2): 250–1.

—— (1996a) 'Welcome to the Network…: Editorial', *The Enquirer*, Summer: 1.

—— (1996b) 'Editorial', *The Enquirer*, Autumn: 1–2.

—— (1997) *Reflective Action Planning for Teachers: A Guide to Teacher-led School and Professional Development*, London: David Fulton.

Frost, D., Durrant, J. and Harrison, J. (1999) *Towards Redefining Research Partnerships Between HEIs and Schools and LEAs*, paper presented at BERA.

Fullan, M. (1991) *The New Meaning of Educational Change*, London: Cassell.

—— (1993) *Change Forces*, London: Falmer Press.

—— (1999) *Change Forces, The Sequel*, London: Falmer Press.

Fullan, M. and Hargreaves, A. (1992) *What's Worth Fighting For In Your School*, Buckingham: Open University Press.

Ganderton, P. (1991) 'Subversion and the Organization: Some Theoretical Considerations', *Educational Management and Administration* 19: 30–6.

Gardner, H. (1993) *Frames of Mind: The Theory of Multiple Intelligences*, London: Fontana.

Georgiades, N.J. and Phillimore, L. (1975) 'The Myth of the Hero-innovator and Alternative Strategies for Organizational Change', in C. Keirnan and F. Woodford (eds), *Behaviour Modification with the Severely Retarded*, Elsevoir Excerpta Medica, 313–19.

Giddens, A. (1984) *The Constitution of Society*, Cambridge: Polity Press.

Gipps, C.V. (1994) *Beyond Testing: Towards a Theory of Educational Assessment*, London: Falmer Press.

Goldstein, H. (1998) 'Yes, but...', *Improving Schools* 1(2): 33–4.

Goodlad, J. (1977) *Networking and Educational Improvement: Reflections on a Strategy*, paper written for the Networking Conference, NIE's School Capacity for Problem Solving Group, Washington, DC: National Institute of Education.

Goodson, I. (1991) 'Sponsoring the Teacher's Voice: Teachers' Lives and Teacher Development', *Cambridge Journal of Education* 21(1): 35–45.

—— (1992) 'Sponsoring the Teacher's Voice', in A. Hargreaves and M. Fullan (eds), *Understanding Teacher Development*, London: Cassell.

—— (1994) *Studying Curriculum*, Buckingham: Open University Press.

Gray, J., Hopkins, D., Reynolds, D., Wilcox, B., Farrell, A. and Jesson, D. (1999) *Improving Schools: Performance and Potential*, Buckingham: Open University Press.

Habermas, J. (1981) *Theorie des kommunikativen Handelns*, Frankfurt: Suhrkamp.

Halsey, A.H. (1992) *The Decline of Donnish Dominion*, Oxford: Clarendon Press.

Hargreaves, A. (1994) *Changing Teachers, Changing Times: Teachers' Work and Culture in the Postmodern Age*, London: Cassell.

—— (1995) 'Beyond Collaboration: Critical Teacher Development in the Postmodern Age', in J. Smyth (ed.), *Critical Discourses on Teacher Development*, London: Cassell, 149–79.

—— (1996) 'Contrived Collegiality: The Micro-Politics of Teacher Collaboration', in M. Bennett, M. Crawford and C. Riches (eds), *Managing Change in Education*, Buckingham: Open University Press, 80–94.

—— (1997) 'From Reform to Renewal: A New Deal for a New Age', in A. Hargreaves and R. Evans (eds), *Beyond Educational Reform: Bringing Teachers Back In*, Buckingham: Open University Press, 105–25.

Hargreaves, A. and Evans, R. (eds) (1997) *Beyond Educational Reform: Bringing Teachers Back In*, Buckingham: Open University Press.

Hargreaves, D.H. (1996) *Teaching as a Research-based Profession: Possibilities and Prospects*, Teacher Training Agency Annual Lecture.

—— (1998) 'The Knowledge-Creating School', paper presented to Symposium on Educational Research – New Directions? at the Annual Conference of the British Educational Research Association, Queens University, Belfast.

Hargreaves, D.H. and Hopkins, D. (1991) *The Empowered School*, London: Cassell.

—— (1994) 'Introduction', in D.H. Hargreaves and D. Hopkins (eds), *Development Planning for School Improvement*, London: Cassell.

Hargreaves, D.H., Hopkins, D. and Leask, M. (1991) *The Empowered School: The Management and Practice of Development Planning*, London: Cassell.

References

Hillman, I. and Stoll, L. (1994) 'Understanding School Improvement', *School Improvement News Research Matters No. 1*, London: Institute of Education, University of London.

Holden, G. (1998) 'One Year On...', *The Enquirer*, Summer: 14–15.

Holly, P. (1984) 'Action Research: A Cautionary Note', *CARN Bulletin No 6*, Cambridge: Cambridge Institute of Education.

Hopkins, D. (1987) *Improving the Quality of Schooling*, Lewes: Falmer Press.

—— (1989) 'Identifying INSET Needs: A School Improvement Perspective', in R. McBride (ed.), *The In-service Training of Teachers*, Lewes: Falmer Press, 84–98.

—— (1996) 'Towards a Theory for School Improvement', in J. Gray et al. (eds), *Merging Traditions: The Future of Research on School Effectiveness and School Improvement*, London: Cassell, 30–50.

Hopkins, D., West, M. and Ainscow, M. (1996) *Improving the Quality of Education for All: Progress and Challenge*, London: David Fulton.

Hopkins, D., West, M., Ainscow, M., Harris, A. and Beresford, J. (1997) *Creating the Conditions for Classroom Improvement: A Handbook of Staff Development Activities*, London: David Fulton.

Hoyle, E. (1986) *The Politics of School Management*, London: Hodder and Stoughton.

Johnston, S. (1994) 'Is Action Research a "Natural" Process?', *Educational Action Research* 2: 39–48.

Kolb, D.A. (1984) *Experiential Learning: Experience as the Source of Learning and Development*, Englewood Cliffs, NJ: Prentice-Hall.

Learmonth, J. (1997) 'Reflecting on Reflection in Professional Development', *The Enquirer*, Autumn: 1, 14.

—— (1999) 'In My View...', Report on ICSEI 99, *Improving Schools* 2(1): 24–5.

Lieberman, A. and Grolnick, M. (1996) 'Networks and Reform in American Education', *Teachers College Record* 98: 7–45.

Lieberman, A. and McLaughlin, M. (1992) 'Networks for Educational Change: Powerful and Problematic', *Kappan* 73: 673–7.

MacBeath, J. (1999) *Why Schools Must Speak for Themselves*, London: Routledge.

MacDonald, B. (1998) *Lawrence Stenhouse Memorial Lecture*, annual conference of the British Educational Research Association, Queens University, Belfast.

MacGilchrist, B., Myers, K. and Reed, J. (1997) *The Intelligent School*, London: Paul Chapman.

MacLure, M (1989) 'Anyone for INSET? Needs Identification and Personal/Professional Development', in R. McBride (ed.), *The In-service Training of Teachers*, Lewes: Falmer Press.

Marlow, E. (1999) 'Withdrawal Symptoms: A Case Study of the Teaching Strategies Employed to Develop the Independent Learning and Metacognitive Skills of a Group of Pupils with Special Educational Needs in a Mainstream School', unpublished MA dissertation, Canterbury Christ Church University College.

McBride, R. (ed.) (1989) *The In-service Training of Teachers*, Lewes: Falmer Press.

McEwen, A. and Thompson, W. (1997) 'After the National Curriculum: Teacher Stress and Morale', *Research in Education* 57.

McIntyre, D. (1998) 'The Usefulness of Educational Research: An Agenda for Consideration and Action', in J. Rudduck and D. McIntyre (eds), *Challenges for Educational Research: New BERA Dialogues*, London: Paul Chapman Publishing, 188–206.

McLaughlin, M. (1990) 'The Rand Change Agent Study Revisited: Macro Perspectives, Micro Realities', *Educational Researcher* 19(9): 11–16.

—— (1997) 'Rebuilding Teacher Professionalism in the United States', in A. Hargreaves and R. Evans (eds), *Beyond Educational Reform: Bringing Teachers Back In*, Buckingham: Open University Press, 77–93.

Mortimore, P., Sammons, P., Stoll, L., Lewis, D. and Ecob, R. (1988) *School Matters: The Junior Years*, Wells: Open Books.

Nisbet, J. and Shucksmith. J. (1986) *Learning Strategies*, London: Routledge and Kegan Paul.

Nixon, J. (1992) 'The Accreditation of Curriculum Development: Enhancing the Process of Reflection through Accreditation: A New Partnership Between Schools and Higher Education', unpublished MA dissertation, Canterbury Christ Church University College.

—— (1996) 'Professional Identity and the Restructuring of Higher Education', *Studies in Higher Education* 21: 5–16.

—— (1996) 'Teaching At the Crossroads', *The Enquirer*, Autumn: 1.

Nixon, J., Martin, J., McKeown, P. and Ranson, S. (1996) *Encouraging Learning: Towards a Theory of the Learning School*, Buckingham: Open University Press.

Parker, A. (1977) 'Networks for Innovation and Problem Solving and Their Use for Improving Education: A Comparative Overview', unpublished manuscript, School Capacity for Problem Solving Group, Washington, DC: National Institute of Education.

Parlett, M. and Hamilton, D. (1972) *Evaluation as Illumination: A New Approach to the Study of Innovatory Programmes*, Occasional Paper No. 9, Edinburgh: Centre for Research in the Educational Sciences.

Parsons, C. (1999) *Education, Exclusion and Citizenship*, London: Routledge.

Parsons, S. (1997) 'Managing to Make Things Happen', unpublished MA dissertation, Canterbury Christ Church University College.

Peters, R.S. (1959) *Authority, Responsibility and Education*, London: Allen and Unwin.

Pring, R. (1984) 'Confidentiality and the Right to Know', in C. Adelman (ed.), *The Politics and Ethics of Evaluation*, London: Croom Helm.

Ranson, S., Martin, J. and Nixon, J. (1997) 'A Learning Democracy for Cooperative Action', *Oxford Review of Education* 23: 117–131.

Reed, J. and Learmonth, J. (1999) 'From Reflective Practice to Revitalised Accountability: Can School Improvement Help?' paper presented at ICSEI '99, San Antonio, Texas, USA.

Reynolds, D. (1994) 'School Effectiveness and Quality in Education', in P. Ribbins and E. Burridge (eds), *Improving Education: Promoting Quality in Schools*, London: Cassell.

—— (1999) 'It's the Classroom, Stupid!', *Times Educational Supplement*, 28 May.

Reynolds, D. and Sullivan, M. (1979) 'Bringing Schools Back In', in L. Barton (ed.), *Schools, Pupils and Deviance*, Driffield: Nafferton Books, 43–58.

Reynolds, D., Bollen, R., Creemers, B., Hopkins, D., Stoll, L. and Lagerweij, N. (1996) *Making Good Schools: Linking School Effectiveness and School Improvement*, London: Routledge.

Rozenholtz, R. (1989) *The Teachers' Workplace: The Social Organization of Schools*, New York: Longman.

References

Rudduck, J. (1985) 'A Case for Case Records?: A Discussion of Some Aspects of Lawrence Stenhouse's Work in Case Study Methodology', in R. Burgess (ed.), *Strategies of Educational Research*, Lewes: Falmer Press, 101–19.

—— (1988) 'The Ownership of Change as a Basis for Teachers' Professional Learning', in J. Calderhead (ed.), *Teachers' Professional Learning*, Lewes: Falmer Press, 205–22.

—— (1991) *Innovation and Change*, Milton Keynes: Open University Press.

Rutter, M., Maughan, B., Mortimore, P. and Ouston, J. (1979) *Fifteen Thousand Hours: Secondary Schools and Their Effects on Schoolchildren*, Shepton Mallet: Open Books.

Rylatt, G. (1997) 'Towards a Tutorial System', unpublished post-graduate diploma dissertation, Canterbury Christ Church University College.

Sammons, P., Hillman, J. and Mortimore, P. (1995) *Key Characterisitics of Effective Schools: A Review of School Effectiveness Research*, report by the Institute of Education for the Office of Standards in Education, London: Institute of Education.

Schon, D. (1983) *The Reflective Practitioner: How Professionals Think in Action*, London: Avebury.

Senge, P.M. (1990) *The Fifth Discipline*, New York: Doubleday.

Sikes, P. (1992) 'Imposed Change and the Experienced Teacher', in M. Fullan and A. Hargreaves (eds), *Teacher Development and Educational Change*, London: Falmer Press, 36–55.

Simons, H. (1996) 'The Paradox of Case Study', in *Cambridge Journal of Education* 26(2): 225–40.

Skoyles, P. (1998a) 'Introducing a Vocational Course for Lower Ability Students into an Academic Sixth Form', unpublished MA dissertation, Canterbury Christ Church University College.

—— (1998b) 'Using the Internet for Research: A Beginner's Experience', *The Enquirer*, Summer: 18.

—— (1999) 'Learning Through Enquiry: Reflections on Five Years as a Teacher Researcher', *The Enquirer*, Spring: 12–13.

Smith, G. (1999) untitled, unpublished portfolio, Canterbury Christ Church University College.

Somekh, B. (1993) 'Quality in Educational Research: The Contribution of Classroom Teachers', in J. Edge and K. Richards (eds), *Teachers Develop Teachers Research: Papers on Classroom Research and Teacher Development*, London: Heinemann, 26–38.

—— (1995) 'The Contribution of Action Research to Development in Social Endeavours: A Position Paper on Action Research Methodology', *British Educational Research Journal* 21: 339–55.

Southworth, G. (1994) 'School Leadership and School Development: Reflections From Research', in G. Southworth (ed.), *Readings in Primary School Development*, London: Falmer Press, 13–28.

Sparke, J., Skoyles, P. and Durrant, J. (1998) 'Analysis of Critical Incidents: Testing a Framework for Developing Professional Judgement and Improving Practice Through Reflection', *The Enquirer*, Summer.

Stenhouse, L. (1975) *An Introduction to Curriculum Research and Development*, London: Heinemann Educational Books.

—— (1978) 'Case Study and Case Records: Towards a Contemporary History of Education', *British Educational Research Journal* 4(2): 21–39.

—— (ed.) (1980a) *Curriculum Research and Development in Action*, London: Heinemann Educational Books.

—— (1980b) 'The Study of Samples and the Study of Cases', Presidential Address to the annual BERA conference, *British Educational Research Journal* 6: 1–6.

—— (1985) 'A Note on Case Study and Educational Practice', in R.G. Burgess (ed.), *Field Methods in the Study of Education*, London: Falmer Press, 263–71.

Stoll, L. (1996) 'Linking School Effectiveness and School Improvement: Issues and Possibilities', in J. Gray, D. Reynolds, C. Fitz-Gibbon and D. Jesson (eds), *Merging Traditions: The Future of Research on School Effectiveness and School Improvement*, London: Cassell, 51–73.

Strauss, A. and Corbin, J. (1998) *Basics of Qualitative Research: Techniques and Procedures for Developing Grounded Theory*, 2nd edn, Thousand Oaks, CA: Sage Publications.

Sutcliffe, J. (1997) 'Enter the Feel-bad Factor', *The Times Educational Supplement*, 10 January.

Teacher Training Agency (1997) *Proposals for the Future Use of INSET Funds*, London: TTA.

—— (1998) *National Professional Standards for Teachers and Headteachers*, London: TTA.

The Standards Site ://www.standards.dfee.gov.uk/guidance

Times Education Supplement (TES) (1998) 'Beacon Schools get £1.8m', 1 May.

—— (1998) 'Are You, Or Have You Ever Been a Conservative?', 1 October.

—— (1998) 'Head of Year Wins £47,000', 21 October.

Tripp, D. (1984) *Critical Incidents in Teaching: Developing Professional Judgement*, London: Routledge.

Velzen, W. van, Miles, M., Ekholm, M., Hameyer, U. and Robin, D. (1985) *Making School Improvement Work: A Conceptual Guide to Practice*, Leuven: ACCO.

Walker, R. (1981) 'On the Uses of Fiction in Educational Research – (And I Don't Mean Cyril Burt)', in D. Smetherham (ed.), *Practicing Evaluation*, Driffield: Nafferton Books.

Waters-Adams, S. (1994) 'Collaboration and Action Research: A Cautionary Tale', *Educational Action Research* 2: 195–210.

Webb, R. and Vulliamy, G. (1996) 'Impact of ERA on Primary Management', *British Educational Research Journal* 22: 441–58.

Wells, G. (1997) 'Learning About Educational Change', *The Enquirer*, Spring: 13, 16–18.

White, J. (1997) 'Philosophical Perspectives on School Effectiveness and School Improvement', in J. White and M. Barber (eds), *Perspectives on School Effectiveness and School Improvement*, London: Institute of Education, University of London, 41–60.

White, S.K. (1988) *The Recent Work of Jurgen Habermas: Reason, Justice and Modernity*, Cambridge: Cambridge University Press.

Woodhead, C. (1999) *The Rise and Fall of the Reflective Practitioner*, HM Chief Inspector of Schools' Annual Lecture, 23 February 1999.

Woods, B. (1997) 'Invisible Teachers: Extracts From Small-Scale Research', *The Enquirer*, Summer.

Wright, A. (1996) 'A Case Study in Whole School Curriculum Development', unpublished postgraduate diploma dissertation, Canterbury Christ Church University College.

The Authors

David Frost is a member of the School of Education at the University of Cambridge. In his previous post at Canterbury Christ Church University College (CCCUC) he launched the scheme at the heart of this book, instigated the Canterbury Action Research Network (CANTARNET) and was the founding editor of *The Enquirer*, the journal for teachers. As a member of the Cambridge School Improvement team since 1996, he has continued to lead the research which resulted in this book and currently works with schools and LEAs to provide frameworks of support for school improvement.

Judy Durrant is a part-time Senior Lecturer in the Faculty of Education at CCCUC, teaching mainly within the context of the Canterbury Improving Schools scheme (CANTIS). She has played key roles in editing *The Enquirer*, and co-ordinating CANTARNET. She has also worked as a researcher for the University of Cambridge School of Education. Most recently she has joined the management group of the Centre for Education Leadership and School Improvement (CELSI) based at CCCUC, and is developing its regional base at Tunbridge Wells.

Michael Head is a part-time Senior Lecturer in the Faculty of Education at CCCUC and a Senior Consultant with CELSI. Before that he was a head-teacher for twenty-three years. In the early 1970s he made a significant contribution to the development of the Humanities Curriculum Project and other innovations in his role as a Teachers' Centre warden. He continues to play a leading role in the co-ordination of CANTARNET, the teachers' network described in this book.

Gary Holden is a Senior Teacher in an 11–18 Roman Catholic Comprehensive School, as well as an Associate Tutor with CCCUC. He has considerable experience of curriculum development and CPD, and he has been a tutor on the CANTIS scheme for five years. He is currently co-ordinating the editing team of *The Enquirer*. He has published articles on school-based inquiry, and he is currently in the final stages of his Ph.D. on the impact of award-bearing CPD on student learning.

Index